THE QUESTION,

"WAS ST. PETER EVER AT ROME?"

𝔅istorically 𝔈onsidered.

THE QUESTION,

"WAS ST. PETER EVER AT ROME?"

HISTORICALLY CONSIDERED.

BY

AUGUSTUS SCHELER,

DOCTOR IN PHILOSOPHY.

TRANSLATED FROM THE FRENCH BY A CLERGYMAN.

WITH

A short Preface by the Translator.

WIPF & STOCK · Eugene, Oregon

Wipf and Stock Publishers
199 W 8th Ave, Suite 3
Eugene, OR 97401

The Question, "Was St. Peter Ever at Rome?"
Historically Considered
By Scheler, Augustus
ISBN 13: 978-1-4982-8312-0
Publication date 2/22/2016
Previously published by James Nisbet and Co., 1846

PREFACE.

THE following work, of which a translation is here offered to the public, was written by a gentleman well known amongst his countrymen for his classical attainments and capacity for dealing with a subject, which requires, in its consideration, research into the records of history and a critical examination of patristic writings.

It was his intention, originally, in submitting the question, " Was St. Peter ever at Rome?" in a popular form to his readers, to have confined himself to a simple translation of the work of M. Ellendorf of Berlin, entitled, " Ist Petrus in Rom und Bischof der römischen Kirche gewesen," merely adding such explanatory notes as the case might require; but, in the course of his labour, it became evident to him, that the subject was susceptible of much additional matter, not only in the way of explanation, but of completion: the idea was, accordingly, suggested to him of such an examination of the question, as, taking the reasoning of M. Ellendorf for a basis, and including the facts adduced by him, should yet admit of an enlargement of evidence and greater extension of application. The result was the work, of which the following pages are the translation.

The peculiar point of controversy treated by Dr. Scheler is one with which Continental theologians are generally conversant. In England, however, its discussion has been confined to a few, and carried on in such a form as to keep it from the knowledge of the greater portion of Protestants—from all, indeed, who, though interested in whatever relates to the Romish controversy, do not possess the attainments of ecclesiastical scholarship, or an acquaintance with the history of ecclesiastical debate—Scaliger, Salmatius, Frederich Spanheim in one form; Ellendorf, Bost, Malan, in another, have fairly laid the subject before their readers; the question has been treated both learnedly and popularly, and the Protestant of the Continent, if he value his standing as such at all, furnished with the matter which these authors have so amply provided, is, consequently, competent to refute, upon sufficient grounds, the alleged supremacy of the Pope, as derived from the fact of an episcopal chair at Rome held by St. Peter. With us, however, in this land, the case is somewhat different. The circumstances which have unhappily taken place of late within the pale of our own communion, and the energetic attacks of Rome upon Protestant faith, have compelled, it is true, a large portion of the Clergy to acquaint themselves with the reasonings for and against Papal primacy; but the generality of the laity and some of their ministers are still in ignorance of much that lies even on the surface of this hardily asserted, but really baseless dogma. There is, with many, a reluctant admission, that the claim of the Romish Church rests on the authority of Eusebius, and a vague idea that this authority is disputable, but there is also an ignorance of the source from whence material may be drawn for its invalidation, and, consequently, a difficulty in giving to a moral conviction the form of a reasonable certainty by logical deduction.

In the hesitation and want of confidence which this ignorance necessarily creates, the Romish Church finds a weakness which she too often successfully assails with the weapon of bold and hardy assertion—a weapon which she knows so well how to wield, and which, where she has ignorance to contend with, she uses unscrupulously, with little care for the manner in which she comes by it, or where it has been forged, the truth or the soundness of the authority of that which she asserts being, indeed, with her a lesser consideration than the effect to be produced or the end to be gained.

It is a desirable thing, under such circumstances, to furnish the many, who would gladly reply to the assertions of Romanists, but know not how, with the means of doing so; and the following pages have been thought fitted for this end, as placing the whole argument for and against the residence of St. Peter at Rome, in a concise form, before the reader, and as combining, with clear reasoning and fair deduction, from the records of Scripture, the real amount of testimony to be gathered from the Fathers.

The author, as will be seen, does not profess to meddle with any thing but the simple *fact* of this residence, and such matter, purely historical, as an examination of the evidence alleged in support of it necessarily involves. No one, however, can fail to see, that though in itself a historical question, immediate deduction from it, as a fact, proved or disproved, must lead into the fiercely contested arena of Romish and Protestant controversy, where the champions of either faith meet hand to hand and foot to foot. Viewing, as we do, the whole Romish system to be one long, fearful, and concentrated heresy against the power, place, and office of the Lord Jesus Christ; believing the asserted supremacy of the Pope, not only to be an usurpation in the household of God, but the very source from whence flow the poisoned streams of doctrine, destroying all the spiritual life and virtue which they meet with in their course, we have no hesitation in confessing, that we put forth this translation with the hope, that in so far as it may invalidate the fact upon which the Papacy is built, it may, in the same degree, damage the superstructure of which it is the foundation.

If the assertion of St. Peter's lengthened residence at Rome be disproved from historical testimony and the nature of the case, it is clear that the Papal claim to supremacy must fall. If there were no such residence, there could not have been an episcopate of twenty-five years, or indeed any episcopate at all, since the only residence of which there is the least likelihood is one of a very short period immediately preceding his martyrdom. In this case, the claim of the Bishop of Rome as the successor of St. Peter in the episcopate, which that Apostle is said to have occupied, is groundless, and resolves itself into what the concurrent testimony of history has always proved it to be, an unwarranted and unwarrantable assumption.

If, on the other hand, the reasoning adduced by Dr. Scheler against the fact of such a residence should be considered inconclusive in positive proof, the claim to supremacy would not thereby be strengthened. The question would rest precisely where it does at present, without any *direct* testimony in support of its assertion; with an alleged evidence, indeed, but of such a nature, that whilst there is no fact which can be brought forward in direct denial, there are many deductions which may be fairly drawn from it against the proposition it seeks to establish: for it is an evidence which, in its several parts, is at variance with itself, more than doubtful in its source, and opposed to all the probabilities of the case. In the failure of this evidence, the absence of any direct testimony, either to the doctrine or the fact, in Holy Scripture, naturally suggests the question, Whether it is likely that our Lord and His Apostles would have left either the one or the other, involving, as they do, consequences of such grave import to the Church and to the world at large, to be gathered by inference? Whether they would have left them subject to the mercy of tradition and its accidents, the chances of oral and mental infirmity in exposition, or the abuses of human ambition?

It may be said, that the Church has *declared* both the *fact* and *teaches* the *doctrine*, and, therefore, no other authority is needed. To this there are two answers. In the first place, as to the fact. This is a matter purely within the region of historical criticism, and can only be maintained in proportion as there is evidence of its existence. It is not competent to the Church to *assert* the existence of a historical fact, which is either disproved or not proved by concurrent testimony. As to the doctrine: though the Church be God's living witness upon earth, yet the Scriptures are the *record* of that witness: they contain the law of which she is the living exponent, and whilst, during the presence of Apostles, there is no doubt that the teaching of God's children was *viva voce*, and the enunciation of doctrine oral,—that what the ministers of the Church heard from the lips of Apostles, they themselves delivered to their flocks (for the canon of Scripture was not then complete), yet the very existence of that canon, as we have it now, would seem to imply, that from the time of its formation, the Church was no longer in a condition to hold and teach these doctrines traditionally, and that the *record* had become necessary, both for the preservation of such truth as it was proper to hold and the avoidance of such error as was likely to arise. If, indeed, the Church could have abided in the light of Apostolical wisdom—if, indeed, by her faith, she could have retained that discernment of truth from error, that heavenly knowledge possessed by her earlier teachers, which were the special gifts of the Holy Ghost, the written letter of Scripture might not have been needed. We know, however, how soon love waxed cold and faith grew dim; and we have a right to assume from the fact, that the very existence of Scripture, in the form in which we have it, is at once a proof that it was not in the power of tradition to preserve the truth of God undefiled, and that it was in itself intended to be a merciful provision of safety and instruction for that condition which the Lord foresaw. The actual revelation which we possess in that record of all that is requisite for salvation to be known, and good for man to believe, makes it clear, that what is not contained therein, or is contrary thereto, was not contemplated as to be binding on the Church.

The Church may have a right of decision in the application of revealed truths; but it is not for a moment to be supposed that she can teach, as fundamental and important, what the Scriptures do not, in some form, contain—much less can it be believed, that so grave a matter, as that under discussion, would have been left for substantiation to the uncertainties of lettered strife and the conflicting testimony of interested parties. The supremacy of one minister over the whole Church contains, as a doctrine, too many ecclesiastical elements of import, and is fraught, in its developement, with too many serious consequences, to have been left without some explicit warrant in command and authoritative explanation. There is no subject of vital importance, much less of *equal* importance, which has been so left; and the fair conclusion from this fact is, not only that a supremacy, like to the Papal, was never contemplated, but that its assumption is contrary to the divine will.

Infant-baptism is often urged by Tractarian writers as a case in point, as that which, in the silence of Scripture, only rests for its authority on the declaration and practice of the Church. Between this doctrine and that of the Papal Supremacy there is, however, this important distinction—that whilst we have in Scripture a record of the command to baptise, an exposition of the nature of baptism, frequent mention and reference to it, and many data which lead to infant-baptism as a fair inference, there is no mention whatever of any supremacy of one man or minister over the Church universal, no trace or reference to that form of it which the Romish church advocates; for what was said to Peter will not apply to the Pope, and clearly was not understood by his brethren, who had the mind of the Lord, as constituting such a supremacy as is claimed. To say that infant-baptism is administered not on the warrant of Scripture, but on the authority of the Church alone, even were it indisputably true, does not touch the point, because the analogy is drawn between two things, which, in reality, possess no such analogy—between that of which in substance frequent mention is made, and that to which in any form there is no reference whatever. The conclusion drawn, that because in the one case there is something for the Church to decide upon what is written, there is, therefore, equal right in the other to assume what is not in any way revealed, is as illogical as it is groundless.

The supremacy of the Pope either is or is not a doctrine necessary for the Church to hold. If it be, how are we to account for the silence of Scripture concerning it? If it be not, what becomes of the Romish claim?

In the second place we would ask, Is it true that the Church has declared this fact and doctrine? We think not. A section of the Church which writes itself "*Roman*," has indeed done so. That section, moreover, has, to her own satisfaction and upon self-constituted authority, unchurched the Greek, the Anglican, and every branch of the professing Church wherein the baptised are to be found, on the ground that in these branches heresies are held, of which heresies she alone, as she says, is competent to judge. Upon her own shewing she is herself unchurched; for she is, and ever has been, rife with heresy, and this not in the judgment of her enemies alone, but in the continual authorisation in one age of what in another, by the very same authority, she has declared to be heterodox. Judge her by the rule of Vincentius Lirinensis, which rule she constantly enforces,—judge her by the decisions of her own Popes and Councils,—judge her by what she anathematizes in her canons, and yet practises, by what she notoriously holds and yet denies that she sanctions,—judge her by what you will out of the ample material of condemnation which she herself furnishes, and she shall be found unchurched if it be true that for the holding of heresy a Church is unchurched. She has voted herself into a chair whose place and authority have ever been disputed, and with matchless hardihood endeavours to constitute herself Catholic by the exclusion of all that is contrary to her assumptions; but the doing this does not prove the fact. She never yet measured that which is contained within the compass of the *Church of Christ;* she never did, and she never will, in any way exhaust the meaning of the word

"THE CHURCH," as "the fulness of Him that filleth all in all;" and the mind must be indeed of limited spiritual perception which regards her as all that is to be looked for or implied in a word of such wondrous signification and extensive application. It is at once a libel on the comprehensive nature of the Divine purpose, and a proof of little Christian intelligence, to say that the Romish Church is, in her standing, a living exposition of the will of Him who, when He ascended up on high, both foresaw and foreordained the constitution of His body mystical on earth; that she, to the exclusion of all other branches of the baptised, is, and ever has been, that body, for whose incorporation the Holy Ghost came down from heaven, and for the perfecting of whose several memberships special ministries were given.

The Church of Rome is not *the Church of Christ*. She is at best but a branch of it; and if heresy unchurch, as she herself asserts, she is hardly that. Power to declare what is and what is not the truth of God, does not rest with any particular portion of the Church, because the mind of Christ, in its *fulness*, is proper to the *whole body*, and the whole body, in its *visible* form, we hold to be constituted by all professing Christians; and though there may be special ministries (such as was the Apostleship, such as is the Pastorship) for its expression, these never can rightly express it in separateness, or to the exclusion of any one of its memberships, however small. The moment the Church of Rome isolated itself from the baptised, it became a spiritual impossibility that she could either rightly or fully express the mind of Christ in such sort that her decision should be the decision of THE CHURCH. The Romish Church may therefore have declared the fact and the doctrine under consideration. But her declaration is not the declaration of *the Church;* and it is idle to reason that it is, until it can be proved that she alone, and without cofellowship of any, is the Church of Christ. The hardihood of her assertion is only proof of her presumption and not of her right.

The Church has ever ruled, that what is not in some form revealed in Scripture is not to be received, and no such doctrine as the supremacy of the Pope can be found therein. In the earlier ages the Church of Rome did not assume the power which she now claims; and, in later times, other branches of the Church of Christ, more faithful to her calling than she has been, freer from positive heresy than she is, and with a better warrant than she can produce, drawn from the record of Scripture, protest against her claim, and assert her place and power to be unwarranted and usurped.

Into the controversy upon the famous words of our Lord to St. Peter it is not our purpose here to enter at length. Those who desire to see a summary of all that has been said on either side, may find it in Elliott's "Delineations of Romanism." * We may, however, remark, in passing, that the Romish interpretation is contrary to all grammatical construction, to sound theology,

* Edited by the Rev. J. Stamp.

and to the probabilities of the case. "Other foundation can no man lay," says the Apostle, "than that is laid, which is Jesus Christ." But if Peter be the *rock* on which the Lord built his Church, other foundation has been laid, and the dogma is established as false in theology as it is illogical in deduction, that the Lord built his Church on *a man*, on a minister and not a ministry, or, in other words, derived the constitution of His body mystical from the personality of one sinful man. That the Church derived its existence from a personality we know; but then that personality was the personality of Him "in whom the Godhead dwelleth bodily." What He contained in Himself He gave to be held by and manifested in His Church, but in such sort as, whilst it may be true, that that Church is "built upon the foundation of Apostles and Prophets," as being ministries wherein He is declared; it is absolutely impossible that any *one* Apostle or man could so possess in himself all fulness as to be *the rock* on which the Church is built. To suppose such a thing is to suppose the existence (we speak in reverence) of two Christs.

If, however, it be granted that such was really the case that this monstrous proposition is nevertheless true—if it be conceded, for the sake of argument, that impossible as it is in fact and improbable in reasoning, nevertheless our Lord did assert this of St. Peter, what follows? Either that Peter, in becoming the Bishop of a particular Church, lost the position into which the Lord had put him, or that the Pope, in succeeding to the fulness of St. Peter's power, is neither Patriarch nor Bishop, but an Apostle—nay, more, is, in his *personality*, as much a *rock* and foundation of a mystical superstructure as was St. Peter. Either of these propositions is untenable; the one is contrary to all theological truth, the other evidently opposed to fact and sound sense.

An Apostle stood in a ministry whose function was the government of the whole Church, which function was exercised in an unity, because it was that which was attached to a ministry, and not to distinct personalities. The Church might, it is true, be assigned for its better supervision in portions or districts to the several Apostles; but the government of one could not be independent of, or contrary to, that of another, for that would have destroyed the unity which it was the special province of this ministry to preserve, and its especial characteristic to manifest. Nor could any Apostle by any possibility become a Bishop of a particular Church without derogating from his office, since his government was of the Church universal, and not of a particular flock, and his oversight was primarily of Bishops themselves, rather than of their people. If Peter was Bishop of Rome, he ceased virtually (we speak under correction) to be an Apostle. In exercising the lesser function contained in his office, he abandoned the greater. In that case what became of his supremacy over the whole Church? The Primacy of the Apostleship, the government of the universal Church, and the Bishopric of a particular flock, are irreconcileable. It is very doubtful, as a matter of fact, whether any *Apostle* was ever Bishop, in the limited sense of that word, of a distinct Church; and it has been asserted that the James who appears as Bishop of Jerusalem was not an Apostle.* The probability of the case is against the fact of an episcopate of Rome held by St. Peter.

But if St. Peter was actually Bishop of of Rome, and did not in holding this bishopric derogate from his office, then the Pope, as his successor, is what Peter was. He is to all intents and purposes an Apostle. This is, however, impossible, since no man can become an Apostle by delegation, seeing that it was an office to which only the Lord could call and ordain. The very proof and

---

* It could not have been James the Great or the elder, the brother of John, for he was slain before the Council of Jerusalem took place; and the circumstances on which the notion of a bishopric at Jerusalem, held by *a James*, is founded, are related as occurring after this event. Dr. Burton believes him to have been a different person from James the son of Alphæus.—*History of the Christian Church*, p. 54. In this case James, the Bishop of Jerusalem, was not an Apostle.

privilege of it was, that he who stood in it should himself have seen the Lord. The Apostleship cannot be delegated. An Apostle may delegate another for certain work, as Paul did both Titus and Timothy; but he never gave, and could not give, his own office of Apostleship to another, for this comes not by imposition of hands, but by the direct calling of the Lord. Titus and Timothy had authority to ordain Bishops; but those Bishops, though, in a sense, successors of Apostles, were not Apostles themselves, and though possessing powers and functions of office necessary to the preservation and well-being of the Church on earth, possessed neither the capacity nor authority for universal rule, which were the special privilege of an Apostleship.

Peter could not constitute the Pope an Apostle; and if he be not this he is a simple Bishop, and nothing more, and in his succession of St. Peter, if St. Peter was ever Bishop of Rome, could not succeed to that which, by Peter's act, was virtually abrogated,—he only succeeded to the lesser functions of episcopacy, in the exercise of which the rest was abandoned. The most proper conclusion, however, to be drawn from such premises is, that the episcopacy of St. Peter is a fiction; the probabilities of the case are against the existence of such a fact. The actual inconsistency of the Pope's anomalous position with all sound theological reasoning is sufficient to warrant us in asserting, that the confusion which must inevitably result is due to the sin and usurpation of Roman Bishops, and not to the voluntary abandonment of his office by the Apostle to the Circumcision.

Again, it has been justly observed, that if Peter were Bishop of Rome, as well as Prince of Apostles, his successor, in inheriting, *ex officio*, his power and privilege, must have taken precedence of any Apostle then living. Thus for instance, Linus, Cletus, or whoever was the first bishop after the martyrdom of St. Peter, would be superior to the Apostle John. Romanists are compelled to admit this, but as a bishop cannot take precedence of an Apostle, this would tend to prove, were the fact asserted a reality, that the successor of St. Peter truly held the place, and possessed the power and privilege of an Apostle—that, in short, he was an Apostle; and we have endeavoured to shew that this is contrary to all sound theological reasoning, and the whole scope of revelation when touching on the office and work of Apostleship. The Pope cannot be an Apostle, and if, as simple bishop, he could not take precedency of an Apostle, the alleged successor of St. Peter could have had no authority over John; and to whatever he succeeded, could not therefore have succeeded to the supremacy, which it is said that St. Peter, though Bishop of Rome, exercised.

In whatever manner we view this *vexata quæstio*, it certainly receives no solution in any way favourable to the Papal claim. As we have before concluded, one of two results presents itself, either that Peter was never Bishop of Rome, or that, if it be true that he held a primacy in the Apostleship, he must, in becoming bishop, have abrogated, not only his primacy, but his standing and place as an Apostle.

It will, perhaps, be thought that the Pope's successorship of St. Peter in the bishopric is so intimately connected with the whole subject of episcopacy, that whatever invalidates the one must by parity of reasoning affect the other. The questions of supremacy and episcopacy are, however, perfectly distinct. The former rests upon the reality of a single fact which is disputed and nowhere proved; the latter upon the direct command of the Apostles, handed down to us in the record of Scripture, and observed in the universal practice of the Church, of which there is such evidence as no one gainsays—the former is a matter of historical criticism and testimony; the latter is a rule of the Church, part and parcel of her very constitution, existing in obedience to the laws of her spiritual being, as a necessary means under God to her visible preservation upon earth. Titus and Timothy had commandment from the Apostle Paul to ordain bishops. He delegated to them for this purpose his own power and authority, and though it is not very clear from Scripture who after them possessed the like authority, yet the very existence of bishops in every part of the Church, in the times immediately succeeding the Apostles, is sufficient to shew that a succession in episcopacy was a rule of the Church, and not an usurpation. Nor does the controversy as to whether the terms bishop and elder were or were not synonymous touch the question, since the real point at issue, between those who maintain an episcopal succession and those who deny it, is not as to *names* but *degrees*—as to whether there were or were not, subsequent to the departure of Apostles, three orders or degrees of ministry in the Church, by whatever name they may be known. If the bishop be more than the elder, and the elder than the deacon, then there are three orders seen; or if the bishop and the elder be one, still Titus and Timothy stood in relation to them in a higher and distinct order: of this fact there is a distinct record in Scripture. The question of episcopacy, therefore, stands upon very different grounds from that of supremacy. In whatever form of manifestation it may exist, still it is a ministry which the whole Church acknowledges, and which even they, who contemn it, unconsciously in some one of its functions maintain—whilst the supremacy of one minister over the whole Church is neither deducible from divine revelation, nor warranted, either by the universal consent of the Church, or the necessity of the case. What our blessed Lord gave in command and commission He gave to His Church in an *Apostleship*, but not in, nor to *any one man*.

It has been often said and written of late, that Christianity is much indebted to the Papal supremacy for the preservation of so much of unity as yet remains in the Church. There is in this a positive sophism; for the unity which is maintained in the Church by means not ordained by God is not an unity either of life or truth. Christianity cannot, therefore, be indebted for the preservation of that which is for her bane and not her good: much less can she hold herself debtor to that which, in its very existence, is a standing lie, and constant dishonour to the Lord. Whatever unity of life has been maintained does not come from the supremacy of one man, but by the operation of the Holy Ghost, in such ministries and means, as being ordained by the Lord, yet remain in His Church. Whatever unity of truth has been preserved is not, cannot be, owing to the existence of the Papal office, wherein the thing which is solemnly asserted one day is as solemnly denied on another; but is due to the possession of the Scriptures, and the unseen, but powerfully influential, supervision of the same Spirit, who mercifully, amidst so many elements of confusion, cherishes and guards the blessed light of that truth, that it be not extinguished through man's mishandling, nor darkened by the intervention of his gross traditions. This boasted unity is, after all, unhappily, an unity in the holding of dogmas, practices, and rites, which are directly subversive of truth, for the preservation of which Christianity owes less to the Popes than the Popes owe to her for all the error they have taught. This naturally leads us to remark, that in the observation which is so often made, and to which we here allude, there is not only a positive sophism, but an absolute forgetfulness, that the real question is not, what of unity remains through the supremacy of the Popes, but what of unity the Church has lost? What of truth has been perverted? what of positive error has been brought in? Whoever fairly considers the question so amended, will find that the Church has little for which she can count herself a debtor to Papal supremacy, but much, alas! of wrong, of oppression, and of heresy, to complain of, for which her faithful children mourn daily before God, and for the avenging of whose infliction judgment is prepared.

It is clear that the Fathers did not understand any such primacy belonging to St. Peter as that which is now claimed by the Romish Church. Cyprian says, indeed,

"Loquitur Dominus ad Petrum : *Ego tibi dico*, inquit, *quia tu es Petrus, et super istam Petram ædificabo ecclesiam meam*, &c. Et idem post resurrectionem suam dicit, *Pasce oves meas*. Et quamvis Apostolis omnibus post resurrectionem suam parem potestatem tribuat, et dicat, *Sicut misit me Pater, et ego mitto vos, &c.*, tamen ut unitatem manifestaret unitatis ejusdem originem ab uno incipientem sua auctoritate disposuit." But he adds, "*Hoc erant utique et cæteri Apostoli, quod fuit Petrus, pari consortio præditi, et honoris et potestatis, sed exordium ab unitate proficiscitur ut ecclesia una monstretur.*" — *De Unitate Eccles.*[*] Origen also, (in Explic. Gen.) and Eucherius Lugdunensis (anno 440), assert that, at the Council of Jerusalem, there was by mutual agreement a division of the world into districts, in each of which the Apostles should specially teach and have supervision. And

---

[*] Pearson on the Creed. He also quotes, in reference to the same view, Irenæus, Clemens Alexandrinus, and St. Jerome.

in this division they mention, that the *West* fell to Peter and James, whilst to Paul was allotted the whole world. Whatever credit may be attached to this legend, it is clear that its authors had no such notion of a supremacy as Romish theologians maintain.* It is more to the purpose to quote the mutual division of labour, and parity of place, without supremacy of either, which are referred to in Galatians ii.

We are not prepared to assert that St. Peter was never at Rome; we think, though there is no positive evidence to the fact, that immediately preceding his martyrdom he went to Rome, where he had not been before, and there, to use the language of Alstedius (*"pauculos menses vivit non ut episcopus sed ut hospes"*), abode for a few months as a guest, and not as a bishop. Neither do we adopt all the reasoning, into which Dr. Scheler enters, in endeavouring to account for the origin of a tradition so

---

* Alstedius, "Thesaurus Chronologiæ," Herbornæ Nassoviorum, 1637.

long and widely accredited as that of an episcopate of St. Peter at Rome, and a consequent succession in place and power on the part of the Roman bishops. This must stand upon its own merits; but the degree of truth or error attaching to the deductions which he draws from the historical data which he has given are more positively appreciable. To us, as far as regards the existence of the fact of an episcopate at Rome, they are incontrovertible. Some allowance must be made by the English reader for a style essentially foreign, which it was not possible, without an emasculation of the reasoning, entirely to alter in the translation. So much liberty as was necessary to accommodate the *vif* style of Continental thought to the more staid and sober paces of home cogitation has been taken with the original, but no more. And the argumentation is, with very little immaterial alteration, such as it stands in the French work of Dr. Scheler.

Our excuse for offering this translation to the public we have already made. A wanton attack upon an ancient faith; a reckless assault upon a time-honoured institution; an unholy and irreverential handling of sacred subjects; are the very last things with which we would sympathise. To any work, where these were the only, or the chief elements, we would not desire for a moment to lend help: but to separate truth from error; to destroy the corruption which fiction gilds and sets up as an idol for idealistic worship; to clear the holy edifice of Christ's Church from the cumbrous inventions of man which disfigure it without, and from the heresies that defile it within, we deem to be a labour, to which every man, who holds the truth of God to be precious, may set his hand, without fearing the imputation of irreverence, or giving ground to the accusation of Godless wantonness.

No one can look abroad with a careful eye, and think deeply over what he sees, without being convinced, that between the absorption of spiritual life and truth in Romish error on the one hand, and their negation by unscriptural and rationalistic

d

interpretation on the other, the visible Church is well-nigh brought to the pass of choosing between the tyranny of Rome and the lawlessness of infidelity. We do not believe, as is too often said, that she can only escape the latter by accepting the former, and we are firmly persuaded, that the way of avoiding both is by cleansing the truth of God from the corruptions with which human invention has surrounded it. Thus nothing will be left of which Rome may avail herself for unscriptural oppression, nor which the modern infidel, confounding it with the doctrine of the Gospel, may use as a handle in the attack of the truth itself.

In the ninth century certain silver keys were shewn at Rome as the identical keys which had been given to St. Peter by our Lord when He said, " I will give unto thee the keys of the kingdom." The fact itself is doubtless indicative of the darkness of an age which could not exercise faith, save through the grosser medium of sensible objects; but it is also symbolical of the actual condition of a Church which either could give credence to such a fact, or impose it as a verity upon her children. If the heads of that Church believed this fact, where was their intelligence? If they did not, where was their honesty? Something more, however, is expressed by the jugglery of these silver keys (for it is but one instance and specimen of a class of impositions), and that is the inevitable tendency of Romanism to sensualise faith, and reduce the higher doctrines, deeper mysteries, and better aspirations of Christianity to gross and fleshly forms. The exhibition of ponderous silver keys as the identical keys given to St. Peter is in keeping with the gross form in which the Church of Rome enunciates her doctrine of purgatory, and is a fitting index to the nature of her belief in that kingdom whose doors these keys were to open. Hence the worldly power and pomp of her rule, her cuirassiers and her police, her political functionaries and penal condemnations, are all so many clear interpretations of the *true* sense in which she understands her claim to supremacy, in which she believes the real authority and standing of the Church of Christ to be constituted. Instances there may be, and doubtless are, of advanced individual perception in spiritual things, of deep devotion and self-denying piety, within her communion; but no one can fail to see that, as she stands visibly before the world, her whole spirit and polity are framed in a most carnal interpretation of Divine truths, whose very form, whilst it retains a semblance of that truth, destroys all its vitality.

Nor will it suffice to say, that the exhibition of these keys, and popular faith in them, belonged to an age whose darkness is passed away; and that the Romish Church, expressing in herself the condition of the times in which she exists, is as much now a partaker of the civilisation of the day as formerly she was a sharer of its ignorance: for the tendency to fleshly interpretation of Divine truth is inherent in her, is a part and parcel of her constitution, and absolutely necessary to her very existence. It has distinguished her in all ages, and is independent of the modifications which social changes might be supposed to impart. The silver keys of the ninth century, and the holy coat at Treves, the "*médaille dite miraculeuse*," the worship of St. Philomène in France, the newly-imported bones of St. Leon and his waxen image in Belgium in the nineteenth, the whole anomalous position of the court of Rome at this present hour—half soldier, half priest, mingling the tricks of political diplomacy with the assumption of ecclesiastical power, sanctity, and purity—are irresistible proofs that Rome has not derived one particle of light from the clearer manifestation of truth which shines around her, nor learned one lesson for her own good, out of the volume of Divine revelation of which she professes to be the only guardian, or even out of the great book of Divine Providence, which is open to all the world beside.

Nor will the argument so often urged avail her, that humanity needs the medium of sensible objects to lift it up to heaven, and that she only employs them to purify the mind and exalt the affections. The churches of Belgium are full of the noblest works of art and the fairest creations of genius; nothing can be more artistically beautiful than the sculptured and pictorial impersonations of the Lord, the blessed Virgin, and the saints. But what is the fact? Prelate and prince, priest and people, without exception, turn their backs upon these noble specimens of exalted conception and human skill, and prostrate themselves in deep devotion before some miserable image of wood, bedizened and bespangled — a wretched mockery in itself — an absolute idolatry in its worship—a deep abasement of the spirit, the heart, and the mind of every one that falls before it. What elevation of thought and affection to heaven can there be through such a medium as this?

That many have gone over to Rome, and that more are to follow, as it is said, are no proofs in themselves that what we have remarked of the Romish Church is not true. These perversions are of that class of spiritual and moral phenomena which God permits, from time to time, to be seen in the world, whereby we learn that neither human intellect nor learning are in themselves safeguards from the subtleties of spiritual error. They are indications of the generally unsettled condition of all men's minds, and the want of the great master principles of Divine truth in those who go over to the Romish Church, rather than of any positive change for the better in her own condition, or greater truthfulness in her standing. The proof of it is in this, that no matter what may have been the amount of honesty, intelligence, or understanding in those who join her communion, before they join it—they communicate no light, they impart no fresh access of life by their adhesion, but are instantly deadened in spirit and darkened in perception by the cold compressions of the system which they enter. What signifies the cry, "There is no Church beside her?" It is not true; and even were it true that no visible ecclesiastical form could be seen on earth beside her, then better far to shut ourselves up to our individual responsibilities before God, to His mercy in and pardon for ecclesiastical irregularity where there is yet life and truth, than commit ourselves to a priestly domination, which shall impose heresy as a rule, and inflict spiritual death and apathy as a condition. If a condition of ecclesiastical irregularity be, as some maintain, a condition of judgment, still it is one permitted by God, where each may know and learn his own sin; and it is better far, even in this sense, to fall into His hands than to be left to the mercy of a system where the condemnation is sure and the power of spiritual perception destroyed.

We feel it a duty in such times to do all that in us lies legitimately to weaken every claim which Rome cannot build on a scriptural foundation, and contest every fact on which she founds her assumption of a power which she cannot prove; and we therefore present this translation to the public, in the hope that it may shew to its readers what real amount of evidence there is, or rather is not, in support of the Romish claim to universal supremacy.

THE QUESTION,

WAS ST. PETER EVER AT ROME?

HISTORICALLY CONSIDERED.

INTRODUCTION.

I CANNOT deny that the treatise which I now present to the public, although it only professes to be a historical dissertation, partakes somewhat of the character of religious controversy, since it openly attacks a belief spread far and wide, propagated from age to age, and, in consequence, almost impossible to eradicate. It should, however, be remembered, that in this treatise the origin of the Papacy is neither submitted for proof to the sentiment of pure evangelical faith, nor to the examination of absolute reason, much less to the judgment of the sceptic, who rejoices in his freedom from religious profession of any kind. The simple question propounded is this: How far the grounds upon which the Romish Church rests for the maintenance of her power can stand before a sound historical criticism — before a lucid exposition and correct appreciation of the facts which the divers records of the primitive ages have transmitted to us?

This question touches the interests of the Romish hierarchy to the very quick; yet if its claims be justly founded it cannot suffer in its consideration. The faith which is based in truth never fears the light, and is strengthened by investigation; whilst, on the contrary, systems built upon error must perish before the test of examination, and in their fall will only have to accuse the nature of the foundation upon which they have been raised. If, therefore, an isolated event, which, though it has generally been admitted as a fact, has never yet been legitimately elevated by the Church into an article of faith — if such an event should be contradicted by historical evidence, or shewn to be plainly wanting in necessary proof for the maintenance of such serious consequences, as those which have been deduced from the existence of the Roman chair of the Apostle St. Peter, then fault must be found, not with the evil intention of him who examines the subject, but with the weakness of the claim examined and the strength of historical truth. It is written in the book of Esdras, "As for the truth, it endureth and is always strong; it liveth and conquereth for evermore. With her there is no accepting of persons, but she doeth the things that are just: neither in her judgment is any unrighteousness; and she is the strength, kingdom, and majesty of all ages."

The Church herself, by one of her most esteemed members, may be said, in some sort, to have recommended the investigation which is here undertaken. Theodoret, bishop of Cyrus, thus writes:—

"Blind faith is, on the contrary, the source of all the evils and errors of the Church. Of all heresies, the worst and most dangerous is that which in our days lifts its head so high and powerfully, viz. that which, exacting from man, with as much absurdity as injustice, that he should renounce his intelligence and accept his religion without examination, hinders him from ever attaining a living and unshaken faith. What is now called faith is too commonly nothing more than an unthinking assent to dogmas which are without foundation, and which do not rest on any demonstration."

I have not undertaken, in this treatise, the task of examining, Whether at any time a primacy, in the catholic sense of that word, was devolved upon St. Peter? Whether, from the time of this Apostle, a Roman supremacy, much less a Roman episcopate, has existed? Whether the chair of Rome was founded by St. Peter or St. Paul, or by any other? Whether the bishopric or primacy of Rome had, from its very commencement, the extent of power and tendency which it has had in subsequent ages? These several questions have been exhausted by others. For myself, I simply ask for proofs in evidence of this one fact:—THE PRESENCE OF ST. PETER IN THE CAPITAL OF THE EMPIRE.

In seeking for these proofs, I have opened the historical records of the primitive ages of the Church; I have consulted the works of those who have been engaged in the same investigations before me; and it is the fruit of these researches which is presented in the following treatise.

A strong and honest conviction cannot be expressed without some degree of warmth. Our words must necessarily partake of the character of our thoughts. It could not, therefore, be expected, that in treating a subject of such high importance, I should remain cold and indifferent, either to the error which has originated the claims of the Romish Church, or the consequences that must result from their destruction.

The principle *sine ira et studio* may well be applied in a simple exposition, but will sometimes be forgotten in the heat of discussion. It should always, however, be borne in mind, that there is a vast distance between a lawful indignation and a virulent bitterness; and I may venture to hope, that whilst it is not impossible, in the consideration of the subject of this treatise, I may have manifested the one, I have succeeded in avoiding the other.

Whoever is conversant with the history of the primitive ages of the Christian Church, and who has traced the influence, direct and indirect, right and wrong, which Christianity, rightly or wrongly understood, has exercised during these epochs, as well upon isolated individuals as upon society at large, will instantly appreciate all the importance which attaches to the subject here under consideration. As he cannot be a stranger to the history of religious controversy, he will remember the many attacks which, since the Reformation, the grave question of St. Peter's residence or episcopacy at Rome has successively induced against the Roman Catholic system. It is, indeed, the triumph and glory of this great Reformation, and of the spirit of investigation on the part of true Christian faith and right reason to which it has given birth, that the Papacy has been continually and fearlessly asked for the documents of its greatness and the titles of its power.

Cardinal Baronius vainly boasts, that *" nec cujusvis perfrictæ frontis hereticus vel schismaticus (eorum qui ante nostrorum sæculum vixerint) ausus fuerit de eo vel leviter quidem dubitationem movere."* The remark in itself does not render an inveterate opinion one whit more plausible. Cyprian declares, that " a custom which has not truth for its foundation is nothing more than an old error."*

But that which approaches very near to rash-

---

* " *Nam consuetudo sine veritate vetustas erroris est.*"— *Ep. LXXV. ad Pomp*. Oxford edition, 1582. The same Father elsewhere writes: " It is not by the duration of time that the authority of religion is measured." Justin Martyr, *in Tryphonem*, expresses himself in the same sense: " They are but fools who prefer custom to truth."

ness on the part of the learned Cardinal, in dealing with the records of the Church, is the declaring a fact, so often contested, to be *toto cœlo perpetuum*,—clear as the light of day, as never having excited the least doubt, when, for the verification of this very fact, the champions of Rome, deprived of other positive proofs, are under the necessity of intrenching themselves *behind the tradition of ages*. The foundation upon which Baronius hazards such an assertion is, " *The first Popes have declared it; even the Emperors have verified it.*" As to the Popes, they had, it is clear, an evident interest in the declaration. As to the Emperors, no one can consider them either as profound or impartial theologians, and their verification is therefore of little worth.

If such foundations as this be really sufficient for the establishment of a historical fact, it is rather astonishing to find the same annalist elsewhere using caution in his assertions, and writing such a sentence as this, " *Sed de rebus tam antiquis et incertis quid potissimum affirmare debeamus non satis constat.*" Surely he who fears not to admit the Roman episcopate of St. Peter on the faith of Popes and Emperors, should never be embarrassed. He has always a master-principle at hand, an infallible authority to which he can refer for the guidance of his pen, viz. that same tribunal which he elsewhere continually invokes and quotes as sufficient authority on the very subject now before us.

I refrain from giving, in this place, a list—which indeed I have not complete—of all the authors, both Protestant and Romanist, who have written concerning the episcopate of St. Peter. I shall only occasionally cite the works which I have used in my own examination of the subject.

The question is a vital one for the continued existence and internal quiet of the Romish Church. The discussion of it is necessary as well as interesting for every man who seeks after the truth, who contemns usurpation, and who abhors the illegitimate restriction of his intelligence and immortal soul. But again I say it, *quæstio non juris sed facti*. It is by no means any doctrine which the Church has authoritatively sanctioned that I attack; neither is it the Catholic faith, as such, that I seek to invalidate: but since councils, encyclical letters, and all the ecclesiastical *materiel* of which the arsenal of the Vatican is composed, have hitherto left this question without any clear, decisive, and well-expounded solution, it is perfectly legitimate to make it one of historical investigation.

Roman Catholic writers themselves have considered it as one of pure historical fact. The Abbé Jarry, a profoundly learned canon of the very illustrious and princely church of Liége, who has undertaken the defence of the claims which the city of Antioch lays to the foundation of its bishopric by the Apostle St. Peter, makes this very evident, when he says, " That St. Peter was bishop both of Antioch and Rome are two facts *purely historical*, which consequently may be proved, as are all common facts of this sort by the same kind of evidence, and which may be discussed according to the rules that ordinarily regulate the consideration of questions of such a nature. The antiquity and the character of the authors who relate them must be examined, the nature of their evidence fairly weighed, and their several testimonies confronted one with the other. The duties and the rights of criticism are limited to this: every other method is clearly one of prejudice or passion."* M. Ellendorf expresses himself on the same subject in terms still more

* Dissertation sur l'Episcopat de St. Pierre à Antioche. Paris, 1807.

decided in p. 94 of his pamphlet. He writes, "The question of St. Peter's residence at Rome is PURELY HISTORICAL in its character. Not having been affirmed either by the divine authority of Sacred Scriptures, or by any infallible decision of any œcumenical council (the decisions of which, after all, are not infallible as concerns facts which do not appear in the Bible), it evidently belongs to the exclusive region of historical examination: it is, in short, analogous to the question, Whether Alexander was ever in India or in Italy? Never," continues the German critic, "never shall history be arrested and hindered in its investigations by the hierarchy or pretended infallibility of Rome; never will she suffer a dictatorial authority to prescribe to her, without any discussion whatever, her answer to this question concerning St. Peter. Caring little for the dogmas which the Court of Rome loves to cherish, she shall pursue her way and maintain the liberty which is due to science. What if Rome, either of her own impulse, or through the intercession of complaisant councils, deprived of the necessary powers for an inquiry of this kind—what if Rome, we repeat it, may have elevated the traditions concerning St. Peter into the certainty of an historical event? What if she shall have proscribed the writings which assert the contrary? These means are now fruitless. Science will not be deprived of her right to examine into these legends, and she yet possesses sufficient liberty to enable her to pronounce the result, by the voice even of a *Catholic*. This last circumstance is one of the mightiest attainments of modern times. The Catholic Church will be free from the Romish vicarship, which declares itself to be of Christ, and from the absolute despotism which flows out of it, from the instant when the study of history exercised within her own pale shall be constituted an independent power. The day must come when Rome shall yield before it."

It is, therefore, a question purely historical that I propose to treat; and in treating it the inquiries propounded are simply these:—

Whether the only records concerning the life of St. Peter which have come down to us, that is to say, the canonical books of the New Testament, authorise us in asserting, either that he was Bishop of Rome for a period of twenty-five years, or indeed ever resided in this city at all?

Whether the quotations from the Fathers of the Church, upon which the Roman Catholic writers lay so great a stress, are really valid and admit of no dispute?

What, in short, are the causes which have given rise to a legend so long and so powerfully accredited?

It is in this threefold investigation that I now proceed to engage the reader, after having, as a preliminary, clearly stated, in all its import and bearing, the fact itself which forms the subject of discussion.

CHAPTER I.

STATEMENT OF THE QUESTION.

THE Roman tradition concerning St. Peter, to which so many religious writers, of different epochs, have devoted brilliant pages of fervent declamation and serious meditation, has its source in the following facts, alleged on the authority of certain ecclesiastical writers : —

1. Until the year 37 the Apostle St. Peter governed the Church of Jerusalem.

2. During this year he visited Antioch, and there founded a Church, over which he presided for the space of seven years.

3. The second year of the reign of the Emperor Claudius, which is the year of Christ 42, he went to Rome in order to put an end in that city to the impostures of Simon the magician. There he established himself as Pastor, and founded an

episcopal chair, which he occupied during twenty-five years; but,

4. In the year 50, an edict of Claudius compelled him to flee, and,

5. Having returned to Jerusalem, he took his place as president at the first council of the Apostles, held on account of the disputes concerning the necessity of circumcising the heathen proselytes.

6. From Jerusalem he set forth to visit Antioch.

7. Claudius being dead, the Apostle returned into Italy, where he resumed his episcopal seat. On his way he established several Churches in Asia Minor.

8. Again setting forth from Rome, the centre of his labours, he undertook several Apostolical voyages into Africa, Spain, amongst the Gauls, and even into England, there organising Churches, and establishing his disciples as Bishops.

9. At last, in the year 63 (66, 67, or 69), he received at Rome the crown of martyrdom simultaneously with St. Paul, in the reign of the Emperor Nero, his wife having previously suffered the like fate.

10. Before he died the Prince of Apostles,

the Sovereign Pontiff, chose Linus to be his successor, who, in like manner, transmitted the dignity of St. Peter to all the Roman Bishops who succeeded him.

In support of this tradition, which is the true basis, the historical foundation of the primacy of Rome, the following passages are transcribed:—

Eusebius, in Chronico.

" Anno secundo Claudii, Petrus Apostolus quum primum Antiochenam ecclesiam (fundasset) Romam mittitur; ubi evangelium prædicans vigintiquinque annis ejusdem episcopus perseverat." *

Hieronymus, de Scriptoribus Ecclesiasticis in Petro.

" Petrus, post episcopatum Antiochensis ecclesiæ et prædicationem dispersionis eorum, qui de circumcisione crediderunt in Ponto, Galatia, Cappadocia, Asia, Bithynia, secundo Claudii anno ad expugnandum Simonem Magum Romam pergit, ibique vigintiquinque annis cathedram sacerdotalem tenuit, usque ad ultimum annum Neronis." †

* Editio Tho. Basson. Lugdun. 1506.
† The Romish tradition concerning St. Peter rests chiefly

S. Leo, Sermo in Nativitatem Apostolorum.

"Cum duodecim Apostoli, accepta per Spiritum Sanctum omnium locutione linguarum, imbuendum evangelio mundum distributis sibi terrarum partibus suscepissent: beatissimus Petrus, princeps

on the two passages from Eusebius and Jerome above quoted. It is curious to observe the degree of confidence which these two authors inspire in the Romish Church, when there is question of the solidity of their assertions.

Baronius declares, concerning the Bishop of Cæsarea, without the least reserve (*Præfat. in Tom. I. Annal. Eccles.*):

"*Ecce enim Eusebius,* ...... *Arianismo semel male imbutus* ...... *multa mentitur est.*" In another place (*ad an.* 324, xlviii.) he says, "*Necessario compellimur affirmare Eusebium dolo malo esse de Constantino tam falso locutum.*" Another Romanist exclaims, "*An non etiam absurdum est, ut qui infidelis ecclesiæ fuerit, ei fidem ecclesia in rebus ecclesiasticis habeat ?*" — MELCH. CANI, *Loc. Theol.* Lib. xi. cap. vi. p. 380, Salmant. 1563. Lastly, a member of the Inquisition cuts the matter short by the assertion, "*Nec curandum est de opinione et historiâ Eusebii.*"—A. PARAMO, *de Origine et Progressu Off. S. Inquis.* p. 436, Matriti, 1598.

Jerome has not met with better treatment from those who call themselves defenders of the Catholic faith; we offer one from the many proofs which might be adduced. "*Ego, et ingenue fatear,*" says the Dominican Canus, "*plus uno summo pontifici crederem, in his quæ fidei mysteria tangunt, quam mille Augustinis, Hieronymis, Gregoriis;*" which is simply saying, that the testimony of Jerome and others is a thousand times inferior to the *dictum* of the Holy Father.

Apostolici ordinis, ad arcem Romani destinatur imperii : ut lux veritatis, quæ in omnium gentium revelabatur salutem, efficacius se ab ipso capite per totum mundi corpus effunderet. Cujus autem nationis homines in hac urbe non essent, aut quæ unquam gentes ignorarent, quod Roma didicisset ? Hic conculcandæ philosophiæ opiniones: hic confutandi dæmonum cultus : hic omnium sacrilegorum destruenda impietas, ubi diligentissima superstitione habebatur collectum quicquid usquam fuit vanis erroribus institutum. Ad hanc ergo urbem, tu beatissime Apostole Petre, venire non metuis et consorte tuæ gloriæ Paulo Apostolo aliarum adhuc ecclesiarum ordinationibus occupato, silvam istam frementium bestiarum, et turbulentissimæ profunditatis oceanum, constantior quam cum supra mare gradereris, ingrederis. Nec mundi dominam times Romam, qui in Caiaphæ domo expaveras sacerdotis ancillam. Numquid autem judicio Pilati aut sævitia Judæorum minor erat vel in Claudio potestas, vel in Nerone crudelitas? Vincebat ergo materiam formidinis vis amoris; nec æstimabas terrori cedendum, dum horum saluti consulis quos susceperas alendos . . . . Jam populos, qui ex circumcisione crediderant, erudieras: jam Antiochenam ecclesiam, ubi primum Christiani dignitas est orta, fundaveras. Jam Pontum, Galatiam, Cappadociam, Asiam atque Bithyniam legibus evangelicæ prædicationis impleveras: nec aut dubius de proventu operis aut de spatio hujus ignarus ætatis, trophæum crucis Christi Romanis arcibus inferebas."

The Jesuit Costerus (who died at Brussels in 1619), in his famous "Enchiridion," establishes the privileges of Rome on the following facts.*

"B. Petrum Apostolum Romam Antiochia migrasse, et quidem divino jussu, ibique mortem oppetiisse, non solum Marcellus Pontifex, martyr (qui Petri sedem, domino jubente, Romam translatam esse scribit) et Egesippus Apostolis vicinus atque B. Ambrosius testes sunt locupletes . . . . . Verum (quantumvis pertinaciter omnes omnium temporum historias infitientur hæretici) scriptores tum historici, tum ecclesiæ doctores, B. Petrum Romæ et sedisse, et martyrio cum B. Paulo coronatum fuisse, diserte affirmant.

* Enchiridion Controversiarum Principuarum Nostri Temporis de Religione, Authore Franc. Costero, Turnoni, 1591, p. 123.

Testantur hoc quoque eorum sacri cineres, qui non alibi, quam Romæ asservantur et loca passionum B. Pauli ad Tres Fontes, B. Petri in Vaticano. Est igitur Petri successor Pontifex Romanus, seu veteris Romæ, non Constantinopoleos, seu novæ Romæ, ubi Petrus nunquam sedit . . . . . non item Alexandriæ, ... non denique Hierosolymorum, etc. Hoc idem fatentur patres et historici Irenæus, Eusebius, Augustinus, Optatus, &c. qui dum seriem Romanorum Pontificum recensent, omnes a B. Apostolo ordiuntur. D. Cyprianus, Hieronymus, Ambrosius, Athanasius, Romanam sedem Petri Cathedram, Ecclesiarum matrem: Romanum Pontificem, Piscatoris Petri successorem, et Rectorem Ecclesiæ, quæ est Domus Dei, appellant."

Lastly, not to multiply these quotations, the celebrated Jesuit Maimbourg (who died in 1686) thus expresses himself on this subject, in his "Traité Historique de l'Etablissement et des Prérogatives de l'Eglise de Rome et de ses Evêques," published at Paris, 1685.

" But the Angel released him from the hands of Herod, and delivered him from prison. After which this Apostle returned into Asia Minor, where he passed the greater part of this year 44, instructing the faithful, and establishing Churches in Cappadocia, Galatia, Pontus, and Bithynia; from thence, having embarked for Rome according to the command which he received from the Holy Ghost, he reached it towards the end of this second year of Claudius, as all the most ancient authors who have written concerning St. Peter agree in stating.

"It was in this, the capital of the empire of the world, that, after having converted Jews and Gentiles sufficient in number to found a Church, he established, in the year following, which was the 45th of Christ, his pontifical chair, leaving that of Antioch to Evodius. This chair he held till his martyrdom, which took place in the year 69, being the 13th of the reign of Nero. Thus, counting from 39 to 45, we shall find a period of about seven years for the seat of St. Peter at Antioch, and from 45 to 69, in which year he was martyred, we shall have the twenty-five years of his episcopate at Rome. . . . . . St. Peter, however, as no one had preached the Gospel at Rome before him, dwelt there seven years, until the year 51, when he was constrained to leave it in consequence of the edict of the Emperor Claudius, which banished the Jews. This compelled him to return into Asia, and it is certain that he was again at Antioch, where he had a great altercation with St. Paul, either before or after the Apostolic Council, which was held that same year at Jerusalem, and at which he assisted.

"Now, as after this council St. Peter could not return to Rome during the life of the Emperor who had banished him from it, and as almost all the other Apostles had their several jurisdictions in the kingdoms of the East, he employed this time in going and proclaiming the Gospel to the nations of the West, even the most distant, for some have written that he went as far as England. So that neither when St. Paul wrote from Corinth (and not from Ragusa) to the Romans in the year 58, nor during the following year, when he was led a prisoner to Rome, nor during the two succeeding years until 61, whilst he remained in that city, had St. Peter returned thither. Nothing, therefore, can be concluded from the silence of St. Paul, who does not mention St. Peter any more than he does St. Luke, who, nevertheless, was with St. Paul at Rome."

We must remark that the chronology of Maimbourg does not agree with the general tradition. That tradition is the one which appears in the commencement of this chapter. The facts are, however, the same, and the Jesuit has only surpassed other writers in his skill in reconciling them one with the other, and making their authenticity appear more plausible.

It would have been useless to have proceeded far into the chaos of chronological systems advanced by different authors on the subject of the Apostle Peter. Their very diversity shews the great difficulty of giving any degree of probability to the facts asserted by the defenders of the privileges of Rome.

The chronological question is, doubtless, an essential part of the discussion; but it is not wished to extend this work unnecessarily by examining the degrees of probability, more or less, attaching to different chronologies. That which is here established, and on which particular stress is laid, does not rest for its maintenance on the refutation of others, but on its own intrinsic value. As for the rest, the steps of a Roman Catholic writer have been principally followed, whose accurate criticism the Court of Rome has

STATEMENT OF THE QUESTION. 23

always dreaded, and whose death, two years ago, has hindered him from taking a part in that struggle, so full of import for the future, which has recently arisen in different States of Germany. M. Ellendorf, Professor of the University of Berlin, is here alluded to, whose numerous works on Church history are as much distinguished by the vast erudition displayed in their compilation as by that grave and profound spirit of thought which characterises the German mind.

The statements which have been quoted above will now be compared with the relation contained in the canonical books of the New Testament of the life, labours, and Apostolic travels of St. Peter.

CHAPTER II.

**EVIDENCE OF THE CANONICAL BOOKS OF THE
NEW TESTAMENT.**

In order to trace the history of the Apostle St. Peter subsequent to the feast of Pentecost (in the year 33 after Christ), it is only necessary to follow with attention and without prejudice the simple relation given in the Acts of the Apostles by St. Luke, the disciple and companion of St. Paul, and to combine with this evidence an important chronological datum furnished by St. Paul in the Epistle to the Galatians.

In doing this the first thing to determine is the epoch of the principal events that mark the first years of the Apostolic times, viz. the martyrdom of St. Stephen, the conversion of St. Paul, and the first Apostolic Council held at Jerusalem. The question whether St. Peter could have left for Rome the second year of the reign of Claudius will then be immediately cleared up.

The death of Stephen must have taken place, if the greater part of Roman Catholic writers are to be believed, at the furthest, eight months after the feast of Pentecost. This supposition is impossible. All that is related in the third, fourth, fifth, and sixth chapters of the Acts must, according to this hypothesis, be comprised within so short a space of time that common sense forbids us to admit it.

Even the maxim of Baronius for this once is in our favour: *" Certum est, Lucam in scribendis Actis Apostolorum illud iniisse consilium, ut res quibus præsens non adfuit vel omnino silentio obvolutas relinqueret,* VEL PLURIMUM ANNORUM SPATIA UNIUS FERE PERIODI SENTENTIA PERFERRET: *quibus vero interfuit cunctas singillatim atque exacte conscriberet."* *

The great number of facts mentioned, with more or less detail in the chapters already quoted, compels us to enlarge the space of time that separates the feast of Pentecost from the death of the first martyr. The multiplied periods in the sentences which we meet with, indicated by particles,

* Ad. Ann. 39, xii.

whose meaning cannot escape any one in the least degree acquainted with Greek, prove a manifest and distinct separation between the several events related. Let us retrace them as briefly as possible. After having recounted in the second chapter, from the 1st to the 41st verse, the outpourings of the Holy Ghost on the day of Pentecost, and the miraculous result of St. Peter's preaching, viz. the conversion of about three thousand souls, St. Luke thus proceeds:

" 42. And they continued stedfastly in the Apostles' doctrine and fellowship, and in breaking of bread and in prayers.

" 43. And fear came upon every soul: and many wonders and signs were done by the Apostles.

" 44. And all that believed were together, and had all things common;

" 45. And sold their possessions and goods, and parted them to all men as every man had need.

" 46. And they continuing daily with one accord in the temple, and breaking bread from house to house, did eat their meat with gladness and singleness of heart.

" 47. Praising God, and having favour with all

the people. And the Lord added to the Church daily such as should be saved."

Clearly, this is neither the history of some weeks nor yet of some months, but the history of the organisation and consolidation of a whole society. When St. Luke wrote these lines he had before his mind, without doubt, an entire epoch.

The third chapter, and the fourth, from the 1st to the 31st verses, comprise the recital of the miraculous cure of a lame man by St. Peter; of the exhortations to the people by which this act was accompanied; of the result of this discourse, viz. the conversion of about five thousand persons: of the imprisonment of St. Peter and John, their appearance before the Jewish council and subsequent release. Now the mention (iv. 6) of the pontificate of Annas enables us to assert that Caiaphas having ceased to be high-priest, the events which are here related must have taken place, at the very least, in the year following the feast of Pentecost.

Chapter iv. verse 34, carries us anew into the midst of this congregation of primitive Christians, whose numbers increased in so wondrous a manner. It is there said, "As many as were possessors of lands or houses sold them, and brought the prices of the things that were sold, and laid them down at the Apostles' feet: and distribution was made unto every man according as he had need." The example of a man of Cyprus is even cited, who having land (most probably in Cyprus) sold it, and brought the money and laid it at the Apostles' feet. Certainly this recital is not the recital of the events of a few weeks. These various operations of the sale of estates, situated some of them out of Palestine, of the investing of the proceeds into one common fund and its ultimate distribution, could not be accomplished in so short a space as certain writers would have us believe.

In the fifth chapter mention is made of the sin of Ananias and Sapphira his wife, and of their punishment. Then St. Luke sums up anew that condition of the Church which followed these circumstances by saying:

"12. And by the hands of the Apostles were many signs and wonders wrought among the people."

"14. And believers were the more added to the Lord, multitudes both of men and women."

"16. There came also a multitude out of the cities round about unto Jerusalem," &c.

The verses 17 and following speak of a second imprisonment of the Apostles by the high-priest and the Sadducees, and of their marvellous deliverance out of prison. The chapter finishes by saying, "And daily in the temple and in every house they ceased not to teach and preach Jesus Christ."

Lastly, the institution of the deaconship, recorded in the sixth chapter, clearly shews us that the Christian community at Jerusalem had arrived at such a point that it became absolutely necessary to establish a special commission charged with the care and oversight of the *widows*. It is difficult to suppose that such a success of the Christian doctrine was the result of a few months. After having mentioned the choosing of the seven first deacons, amongst whom was Stephen, the sacred historian thus continues, v. 7 : "And the word of God increased; and the number of the disciples multiplied in Jerusalem greatly; and a great company of the priests were obedient to the faith."

It is more than probable that between the institution of the deacons and the death of the first among them, a greater space of time than a *few days* must have elapsed; for the verses 8 and following prove to us that this death was not caused by a single discourse or fact, but was the result of a prolonged activity and its powerful effects.

This statement of all the events which preceded the death of Stephen, as St. Luke relates them, and the observations to which it has given rise, naturally leads us then to admit between the day of Pentecost and the death of the first martyr a period of some years instead of months, and proves to us that this death could scarcely have occurred before the year 35 or 36. M. Ellendorf goes so far even as to suppose that the great persecution, by which the punishment of Stephen was followed, could not have taken place till after the death of the Emperor Tiberius (anno 37), seeing that, according to the testimony of Tacitus ("Annales," ii. 85), of Suetonius (Tib. 36), and of Josephus ("Antiq." xviii. 4, 5), although this Emperor was the declared enemy of the Jews, he had nevertheless, as we also learn from the testimony of Tertullian (Apolog. 5), manifested a favourable disposition towards the Christians, and was not likely therefore to have consented to those heavy persecutions of which they were specially the objects after the death of Stephen. Without, however, hazarding any decision on this latter point, we may safely fix the martyrdom of St. Stephen to the year 35 or 36.

The time which elapsed between this event and the conversion of St. Paul can only be determined by a scrupulous examination of the eighth chapter of the Acts. It is the only chapter which comes in between these two events. It is there said, v. 3, "And as for Saul, he made havoc of the Church, entering into every house, and haling men and women, committed them to prison.

"4. Therefore they that were scattered abroad went every where preaching the word.

"5. Then Philip (one of the seven deacons) went down to the city of Samaria and preached Christ unto them."

"14. Now when the Apostles which were at Jerusalem heard that Samaria had received the word of God, they sent unto them Peter and John."

"25. And they, when they had testified and preached the word of the Lord" (and having combated the errors of Simon the Sorcerer), "returned to Jerusalem, and preached the Gospel in many villages of the Samaritans."

As to Philip he went as far as Gaza, a maritime

city in the south-west of Judea; and from thence, in passing by Azotus, he came to Cæsarea. It was at Gaza that he was made instrumental to the conversion of the treasurer of Candace, queen of Ethiopia. All this was accomplished whilst "Saul was yet breathing out threatenings and slaughter against the disciples of the Lord" (ix. 1).

We do not think it therefore rash to assert that some years must have elapsed between the death of St. Stephen and the conversion of St. Paul, the latter of which events probably took place towards the year 39.

Ellendorf confirms this opinion in the following considerations, the weight of which cannot be contested:

1. At the time of the death of the first martyr St. Paul was but a *youth* (νεανιας), as it is said in chap. vii. 58, and, as such, a disciple of Gamaliel, as, indeed, is evident from his own declaration, Acts, xxii. 3. Gamaliel having been the declared enemy of all violence towards the Christians, as appears from the close of the fifth chapter of Acts, it seems clear that Saul, the furious persecutor, must in the interval have broken off all those connexions which attached him to this doctor. Moreover, the Christian of Damascus, Ananias,

describes him as a *man* (ix. 13) (ἀνήρ); and it is by no means probable that the high-priest would have furnished a mere youth with full powers of such a nature as those described in the 2d verse of the ninth chapter.

2. We know that St. Paul, after his first journey to Jerusalem, which he undertook three years after his conversion (Gal. i. 18), went to Tarsus, the city of his birth (Acts, ix. 30); and it was from thence that Barnabas came to take him, in order to conduct him to Antioch, where they laboured together in the work of Christianity for an entire year (Acts, xi. 25, 26). It was during their abode at Antioch that they were sent to Jerusalem with the alms which had been gathered for the relief of the brethren abiding in that city, then menaced with famine. Now this journey coincides with the imprisonment of St. Peter by Herod Agrippa (xii.), and therefore occurred (this date is certain) in the year 45. If we allow the chronology of Baronius and of Noel Alexandre, according to which St. Paul was converted in 34, and came to Jerusalem in 37 or 38, how shall we fill up the period from 37 or 38 to 45? Did Paul remain in idleness at Tarsus during six or seven years? Whilst that, if we fix the epoch

of the conversion to 39, we shall make St. Paul arrive at Jerusalem in 42, go on that same year to Tarsus, and in passing by Cæsarea remain there till towards the year 44. Barnabas calls him to Antioch to be his fellow-labourer in the preaching of the Gospel; and finally, in 45 we shall find him arriving in the company of Barnabas at Jerusalem to be a witness to the imprisonment of Peter under Herod.

Let the probabilities of these two systems be compared and judged accordingly. We think there is little doubt as to which will be preferred, and are firmly of opinion that St. Paul was not converted before the year 39.

According to his own testimony (Gal. i. 18), Paul, theretofore so fierce a persecutor of the disciples of Christ, went up to Jerusalem three years after his conversion, *in order to visit Peter,* and there abode fifteen days. This journey is also related by St. Luke (Acts, ix. 26–30). It took place, according to our calculation, in the year 42.

This fact proves to us that, before this year, which is the second year of the reign of Claudius, Peter had not yet quitted Jerusalem, where the necessity of organising the first Church retained him, unless, indeed, for the purpose of preaching the Gospel in Samaria (Acts, viii. 1, 14, 25). He could not possibly, therefore, in 37 have founded the chair of Antioch, have occupied it during a period of seven years, and after that have gone into Italy in the year 42.

It is not until after he has mentioned the departure of St. Paul for Cæsarea and Tarsus, that the author of the Acts relates (ix. 31), "Then had the Churches rest throughout all Judea and Galilee and Samaria, and were edified; and walking in the fear of the Lord, and in the comfort of the Holy Ghost, were multiplied." The following verse plainly refers to this condition of things, and it is there stated, "And it came to pass, as Peter passed throughout all quarters, he came down also to the saints which dwelt at Lydda," a small town situated at about three leagues distance from the sea and eight from Jerusalem, where he cured a man sick of the palsy. From thence he went, according to the verses 38 and 39, to Joppa, where (v. 39), he tarried many days, and from thence to Cæsarea, the residence of the Roman governors as well as of Herod (xii. 19). It was here that the conversion of Cornelius the centurion took place, as is recorded in the 10th chapter. The Apostle probably remained there some days (v. 48), before he returned to Jerusalem (xi. 2), which was distant from Cæsarea about twenty-five leagues. In combining the distances of the different places visited with the stay, more or less prolonged, which the Apostle made in them, we shall not exceed the bounds of probability in fixing the period of his return to Jerusalem to the year 45.

Nothing yet has announced any journey of St. Peter to Antioch. On the contrary, the 19th verse of the 11th chapter informs us, that " They which were scattered abroad upon the persecution that arose about Stephen travelled as far as Phenice, and Cyprus, and *Antioch.*" Their success determined the Apostles who were at Jerusalem to send Barnabas to this latter city.

The history of St. Luke offers us no details whatever on that which passed during the year 44, following the return of St. Peter to Jerusalem; but the imprisonment of St. Peter, recorded in the 12th chapter, necessarily leads us to believe that the evangelical labours of the Apostle which urged Herod to this act of severity must have been most important; and, as this act passed but a short time before the death of the Tetrarch (xii. 19-24), an event which took place in the fourth year of the reign of Claudius, being the year of Christ 45,* we have just grounds for asserting as a historical truth, that before this period St. Peter had not yet passed the boundaries of Palestine.

Where, then, shall we place the seven years of the episcopate at Antioch attributed to this Apostle both by the Church and the whole mass of Roman Catholic writers? In truth we can find nothing any more than the learned Tillemont,† which will solve the difficulties that arise on all hands against the assertions of those who, even though they reduce considerably the number *seven,* yet contend for the reality of the fact itself, viz. St. Peter's episcopate at Antioch.

---

* Vide Josephus, "Antiq." xix. 8. It is there said that Herod reigned seven years, four under Caius Caligula, and three under Claudius. But Usserius remarks, that from these first four years three or four months must be subtracted, since the Emperor Caligula did not reign four entire years, and that these three or four months must be added to the reign of Claudius.—*In Annalibus,* ed. Lond.

† Le Nain de Tillemont, in his "Notes sur St. Pierre," (Mémoires, tom. i. part 2, edit. de Bruxelles, 1706, p. 739), finds the episcopate of St. Peter at Antioch a very embarrassing subject, and seems disposed to deduce the whole of this tradition from the corrupt source of the pretended "Recognitiones" of Clement, from which some martyrologists have derived what they say of the 22d February.—BOLLANDUS, 22 Fev. pp. 283–6.

Let us, however, examine a little more closely this question, which forms, as it were, the first part of the tradition concerning St. Peter. If this be shewn to be destitute of all historical foundation, the second part of the tradition relating to an episcopate of twenty-five years at Rome will equally lose a great portion of its credibility. We will follow on this subject, which is something more than an accessory, the same order which we have observed in the work at large. We will first consult the authorities in the Bible, and thence pass to the evidence afforded in sacred antiquity.

Here is what the Bible teaches us (Acts, xi.) concerning the foundation of the Church at Antioch, vv. 19–26 :—

" Now they which were scattered abroad upon the persecution that arose about Stephen travelled as far as Phenice, and Cyprus, and Antioch, preaching the word to none but unto the Jews only.

" And some of them were men of Cyprus and Cyrene, which, when they were come to Antioch, spake unto the Grecians, preaching the Lord Jesus.

" And the hand of the Lord was with them:

and a great number believed, and turned unto the Lord.

"Then tidings of these things came unto the ears of the Church which was in Jerusalem: and they sent forth Barnabas, that he should go as far as Antioch.

"Who, when he came, and had seen the grace of God, was glad, and exhorted them all, that with purpose of heart they would cleave unto the Lord.

"For he was a good man, and full of the Holy Ghost and of faith: and much people was added unto the Lord.

"Then departed Barnabas to Tarsus, for to seek Saul:

"And when he had found him, he brought him unto Antioch. And it came to pass, that a whole year they assembled themselves with the Church, and taught much people. And the disciples were called Christians first in Antioch."

Now this is the simple recital in the New Testament of the foundation of the Christian communion at Antioch. There is not a word concerning a bishop, much less of St. Peter. We have seen that the mission of Barnabas took place towards the year 42 or 43, whilst St. Peter went through the churches of Judea, Galilee, and Samaria, and before that this Apostle had passed the boundaries of Palestine.

Even if it be granted that the opinion of the Roman Catholic writers be correct, and that St. Paul was converted in 34, he could not have come to Antioch with Barnabas before the year 38; nevertheless, these writers fix the foundation of the Church at Antioch to the year 34 or 35, and assert St. Peter to have been its first bishop in the year 37. What an admirable deduction! Who we may ask, then, presided over this church from 34 to 37?

Moreover, Baronius, admitting, according to Dion Cassius (ix. in Claudio), that the famine (mentioned in Acts, xi. 28, and which occasioned the journey of Barnabas and St. Paul to Rome) took place in the year 42, ought, to be consequent, to have placed St. Peter at this time as Bishop of Antioch; but it is exactly at this very period that St. Peter was at Jerusalem and imprisoned by Herod. This is a most troublesome *alibi*. But, perhaps, St. Peter might happen *accidentally* to be at Jerusalem when he was imprisoned by Herod. Let us, then, look for some argument of greater weight.

After having mentioned the return of the two Apostles to Antioch (xii. 25), St. Luke gives (xiii. 1) a list of the different teachers and prophets, who were united in this city administering the Church and exercising even a species of authority over St. Paul and Barnabas: not a word of St. Peter!

Whether, therefore, we follow the chronology of Baronius, &c., or our own, based on a free and independent examination of the text of the Acts, numerous obstacles hinder us from admitting an episcopate of St. Peter at Antioch during the years 37 to 44.*

We will not stop to detect all the absurdities to which an anxious desire to reconcile the errors of tradition with the relation of the sacred books has given birth: we will rather examine the tradition itself, for we can well afford to do so

---

* The learned Jesuit Halloix (who died at Liége in 1656), *in Vita Ignatii*, t. i. c. 2, thus expresses his doubts on an episcopate of St. Peter at Antioch from 38 to 44 : " Si ante hæc tempora fuisset Antiochiæ, ibique ecclesiam fundasset, sedemque suam statuisset, S. Lucas, capite xi. Actorum, facta proxime Petri mentione debuisset non tantum de viris illis Cypriis et Cyrenæis loqui, sed multo magis de Petro, si quidem tamdiu ibi fuisset, ut jam tum haberetur Antiochenus episcopus. *Itaque nondum eo venerat.*"

without a moment hazarding the validity of our opinion. The question how the idea of this episcopate ever became a settled belief, may be resolved in the same manner as that which has reference to the Roman episcopate of the same Apostle. This claim is only founded on the ambition of communities, which does not hesitate to use fraudulent means in its gratification. The Bible was opposed to it, the witness of holy tradition then became necessary; but the very men whose writings or words constitute this evidence are themselves liable to error, and in their humility a hundred times acknowledged it.

The passages which are generally quoted are these:—

S. Ignatii ep. 12 *ad Antiochenos:* "Mementote Evodii beatissimi pastoris vestri, qui primus post Apostolos gubernacula vestræ ecclesiæ sortitus est."

But, in the first place, this letter is supposititious, as most learned Roman Catholics and Noel Alexandre himself, who uses it, admit; and, in the second place, it makes no special mention of St. Peter.

Eusebius, iii. 16: "Porro EVODIUS PRIMUS FUIT Antiochiæ episcopus, secundus Ignatius, qui illis temporibus multum hominum sermonibus celebratus fuit."

Far from proving the episcopate of St. Peter at Antioch, this passage witnesses in our favour that St. Peter was not the *first* bishop of this church, as tradition is asserted to declare.

Hieronymus, in Catalogo: " Ignatius Antiochenæ ecclesiæ TERTIUS post Petrum Apostolum episcopus."*

Jerome wrote in the fifth century, a period when nothing but forgery is met with. Jerome may have been deceived in this place, as well as in many others.

Chrysostomus, Homil. de Laudibus S. Ignatii: " Ignatius S. Petro in episcopatus dignitate successit. Nam ut si quis e fundamentis magnum lapidem eruat, alterum omnino parem in ejus loco conatur constituere : nisi velit alioqui totum concutere ac debilius reddere : ita cum Petrus Antiochia esset discessurus, alterum Petro parem præceptorem gratia Spiritus substituit, ne structa jam ædificatio successoris imbecilitate debilior fieret."†

* Paris edition, 1524, p. 278.

† Edition of Paris, 1718, b. ii. p. 597. There is a passage in the same Father which may help us to trace the origin of the claims of the Church of Antioch : " Hæc enim est una etiam

But, in the first place, Chrysostom was, it is well known, a priest of the Church at Antioch at the time he wrote this letter, and was, therefore, doubtless influenced in some measure by the local interests of that city;

Secondly, The saint in this statement is at variance with the assertions previously quoted, which make mention of an Evodius as the predecessor of Ignatius; and it needs such subtle refinements as Noel Alexandre employs on this subject (Dissert. p. 177, col. 2), to reconcile these striking discrepancies; and,

Thirdly, The same preacher uses very different language in his Homily on the 11th of Acts (edit. de Paris, 1837, ix. p. 218) : " Factum est autem, ut totum annum congregarentur in ecclesiam et docerent turbam multam, ita ut cognominarentur primum Antiochiæ discipuli Christiani. Hoc contra omnes adduci potest, quod prima omnium ore tali tanto tempore frueretur : unde et primo isthic hoc nomine dignati sunt. Vide'n in quan-

---

nostræ civitatis prærogativa dignitatis, quod principem apostolorum ab initio doctorem acceperit. *Æquum* enim erat, ut ea, quæ nomine Christianorum ante universum orbem terrarum ornata fuit, primum Apostolorum pastorem acciperet."—Tom. ii. p. 85 c. Paris edition, 1837.

tum fastigium civitatem extulerit, clarioremque fecerit ? Hoc PAULI opus est."

Theodoretus, in Dialogo: Immutabilis: " De illo enim Ignatio omnino audisti, qui per magni Petri dextram pontificatum suscepit."

This passage from the Bishop of Cyrus (anno 457), which does no more than corroborate the fact of St. Peter's stay at Antioch, is in opposition to a passage in the Apostolical Constitutions (composed in the fifth century), vii. 46, which states that Ignatius had been ordained by St. Paul; it is at variance also with the Acts of the Martyrdom of this saint (in the "Acta Martyrum Sincera et Selecta," Paris, 1689, 4), which mention St. John as his master; as well as with the Acts of the Martyrdom of Simon Metaphrastes, where the ordination of Ignatius is attributed to all the Apostles together. Ἱερεὺς κοινῇ πάντων ὁμοῦ τῶν Ἀποστόλων ψήφῳ χειροτονεῖται, καὶ τῶν Ἀντιοχέων ἐκκλησίας ἐπίσκοπος προχειρίζεται. This is a fair specimen of the agreement which is met with in those Catholic writings, which are the sources of the system.

Felix III., in Ep. ad Zenon Imperat. (p.c. 492), only repeats what Theodoret had said.

The *Roman Council* under Damasus states,

"Tertia vero sedes apud Antiochiam Apostoli Petri habetur, honorabilis, eo quod illam primitus quum Romam venit, habitavit et illic primum nomen Christianum novellæ gentis exortum est."

The value of this passage is glaringly manifest. It makes against those who quote it.

S. Leo, Serm. I. in Nat. Apost.: " Jam Antiochenam, Petre, ecclesiam, ubi primum Christiani nominis dignitas exorta est, fundaveras."

Gregorius I. lib. vi. epist. 37 : "S. Petrus firmavit sedem in qua septem annis quamvis discessurus sedit." (Edition of Paris, 1640.)

Now it is in the writings of this author that the figure 7 appears for the first time, and we have already arrived at the seventh century. This assertion of Gregory is, therefore, somewhat modern ; and it is rather too presumptuous to attach so high a value to it.

In short, he who would sustain that St. Peter held an episcopate in the capital of Syria must of necessity be blind to the evidence presented to his mind, and enslaved by prejudice, especially if he moreover contends that such an episcopate endured for seven years. This tradition is nothing more than the fruit of an unholy ambition in the Church of the earlier ages, which, in coveting prerogatives, invented fables in order to obtain them.

We will now resume the interrupted narrative of the biography of St. Peter, and follow the course of events related in the Acts. We left this history at the period of St. Peter's imprisonment under Herod.

We read (chap. xii. 12-17) that, after his deliverance, "he came to the house of Mary, the mother of John, whose surname was Mark;" and from thence "he departed and went into another place." This indefinite expression will hardly permit us to suppose that by this is meant a journey into another country; we are rather led to infer, that he simply withdrew from Jerusalem that he might escape the pursuit of Herod, and that after the death of this prince, who did not long survive the deliverance of St. Peter, the Apostle again returned to Jerusalem, which up to that time had been the centre of his Apostolical labours.

From this period the narrative passes on to the first Council of the Apostles, where we again meet with Peter, without any special authority, without any of the prestige and eminence in superiority necessarily attaching to the dignity which the Roman Church claims for his position. He is there simply represented as taking his place with his brethren, without any assumption of superior power, and in the true unity and lowliness of that Church which, faithful to the will of her Divine Master, yet refused and abhorred worldly honours and titles.*

How shall we fill up the hiatus that occurs between the departure of St. Peter from Jerusalem and his reappearance in that city at the council of the Apostles? Shall we invent a fact? Shall we yield to the supposition, that during the period that elapsed between these two periods, St. Peter

---

* Vide Matthew, xxiii. 8–11. It was not till the fourth century that pious men needed to remind Christians of the true nature and character of the episcopate, and this necessity arose from the disastrous compromise of the Church with imperial power. It was then that Jerome thus wrote: "A bishoprick is a work, and not a dignity; a labour, and not an enjoyment. It is a perpetual exercise of humility, and not a pampering of ambition and pride."—*Epist. Oceano.* Even at this early period the same writer says, "Yesterday a catechumen, to-day a pontiff; yesterday in the amphitheatre, to-day in the Church; at night at the circus, in the morning at the altar."—*Ibid.*

"*Si quis episcopatum desiderat, bonum opus desiderat. Opus, non dignitatem; laborem, non delicias. Opus per quod humilitate decrescat, non intumescat fastigio.*"

"*Heri catechumenus, hodie pontifex; heri in amphitheatro, hodie in ecclesia; vespere in circo, mane in altario.*"

went to Rome in order to create that institution which continually glories in him as its inspired founder? Shall we recur to fictions and to pious frauds, that we may flatter the pride, that we may pander to the ambition, the vanity, or the temporal interests of a sect? We will rather conclude, with more reason and conformably with historical data, that it was exactly at this period that the Apostle Peter commenced the fulfilment of the mission with which he had been specially intrusted. He was, as we learn, the Apostle to the circumcision (Gal. ii. 7); and it is much more consistent with the character of this commission to suppose that he would turn in his missionary zeal towards the numerous communities of Jews scattered throughout the different provinces of the East rather than towards Rome, at that time the stronghold of paganism. Of the details of his labours we know nothing more. Whatever they were, they seem to have been eclipsed in the annals of Christianity by the more brilliant success of him upon whom a mightier task had devolved, that of evangelising the Gentiles. And it is certainly owing to something more than a mere chance that from the 12th chapter of the Acts the name of St. Peter only occurs six times in the canonical books of the New Testament, while that of St. Paul is mentioned no less than one hundred and fifty-six.*

We meet with St. Peter again, as we have just said, at the time of the first convocation of the Apostles at Jerusalem, commonly called the first Apostolic Council. This event is described in the 15th chapter of the Acts, and is thus related by St. Luke : " And certain men which came down from Judea taught the brethren, and said, Except ye be circumcised after the manner of Moses, ye cannot be saved. When, therefore, Paul and Barnabas had no small dissension and disputation with them, they determined that Paul and Barnabas, and certain other of them, should go up to Jerusalem unto the Apostles and Elders about this question. . . . . . And the Apostles and Elders came together for to consider of this matter, and when there had been much disputing, Peter rose and said . . . ."

Now in all this there is not the slightest thing that can give rise to the least supposition of St. Peter's having come from a distance in order

---

* Appel à la Conscience de tous les Catholiques Romains. Par A. Bost. Toulouse, 1841. P. 88, &c.

to assist at this council. Nevertheless, the Romish writers assert that he came from Rome, which place he had been compelled to leave in consequence of the edict of Claudius, who about this time expelled the Jews from the capital (Suetonius, Claudius, 25 ; Acts, xviii. 2). This, however, is pure supposition, and rests upon no historical foundation whatever.

If it be asserted that St. Peter convoked this first council in virtue of his place and authority as Prince of the Apostles, then we ask, Where are the proofs ? Systems of such vast import as that of the Papacy are not constructed on a *probability*, or even on less than that. All that can be certainly gathered from the council of Jerusalem is, that Peter spoke as well as James, as well also as Paul and Barnabas, and nothing more.

It remains now that we fix the time of this meeting.

Paul aids us in this when he says (Gal. ii. 1), "Then fourteen years after, I went up again to Jerusalem with Barnabas, and took Titus with me." All theologians agree in stating that this is the same journey as that related by St. Luke, Acts, xv. 2 ; but it is necessary to ascertain to what event the word "*then*" bears reference,—

whether to the conversion of St. Paul, or to his first interview with the Apostles at Jerusalem? As it would be very difficult, in admitting the last of these suppositions, and in accordance with the detailed recital which St. Luke gives us of the life of St. Paul, to fill up these fourteen years between his first departure from Jerusalem and the period of the council, we think that they should be reckoned from the conversion of this Apostle. Now as we have already fixed this event to the year 39, we must consequently place the council somewhere about the year 53. According to Baronius and others, who hasten the progress of events more rapidly than we have dared to do, and thus gain a period of four or five years, this council took place in the year 48.

For our own parts, in the reasoning which we have followed, we are convinced that Peter had not seen Rome in the year 52 or 53.

After the council had ended, we learn, from Acts xv., that Paul and Barnabas returned to Antioch, and there (ver. 35) they continued teaching and preaching the word of the Lord, with many others also. It was during this last residence of Paul at Antioch that Peter came there (Gal. ii. 11) and provoked those remonstrances from the great Apostle, which so clearly shew the nature of their relation one to another. We gather from the facts here recorded, that Peter, before the year 53 or 54, had not yet quitted the East. On the contrary, we presume that it was in visiting the Jews scattered throughout Pontus, Galatia, Cappadocia, Asia, and Bithynia, that Peter passed by Antioch, the illustrious seat of Paul and Barnabas. We can assert nothing positive, for the Acts by St. Luke teach us nothing more whatever concerning the life of St. Peter.

The more moderate opinions of Pagi and Count Stolberg place the departure of Peter for Rome after the council at Jerusalem, and towards the commencement of the reign of Nero, in the year 54; but even to this opinion we cannot, as will be seen, adhere.

Thus, so far, the result which we obtain from the Acts is, that before the year 54 Peter could not have visited Rome; not only is there no appearance of truth in favour of the assertion that he did so, but positive facts and convincing realities are opposed to it.

From henceforth our reasoning will rest no longer and 'exclusively on the data drawn from the historical book of the New Testament. We now leave the Acts of the Apostles, but the discussion of the subject will not thereby be weakened, it will merely be carried on in other regions.

In default of facts for the support of our conviction, we are about to invoke another argument not less formidable. If facts be silent, then silence itself shall speak. Let us listen to its powerful eloquence.*

The Epistle to the Romans was written, no one can contest it, in the year 58, five years after the Apostolic Council. Now we would ask, In this epistle is there the slightest allusion to any residence, present or past, of the Apostle St. Peter in the city of Rome as ecclesiastical head or bishop, established at that time for sixteen years, or even, according to Stolberg and Pagi, for four years? Is there even the least mention of *any prince* of the universal Church, setting aside all question

---

* This mode of argument is even recommended by the Père Mabillon, in his "Traité des Etudes Monastiques" (tom. ii. part 2, ch. 13). He says, "It is, moreover, very important in criticism to make a good use of the negative argument. This is absolutely necessary in certain positions, in order to destroy mere tales and fables which impostors forge at their pleasure to surprise us. They can only be refuted by the argument negative, although it is a means which may be abused if carried too far."

as to the personality of that prince? On this point, however, we will quote from one who has most ably treated it.

" It is towards the year 58 that Paul wrote his celebrated Epistle to the Romans—to the Romans be it remembered—to those very Romans of whom St. Peter, according to the tradition, must at that time have been a bishop for a period of seventeen years! Behold him, therefore, without doubt, the recognised head of the Church in its principal locality! How is it, then, that we do not find mention of him in all his glory in this epistle? How is it that we do not find the least trace of him? Perhaps he had set forth on some journey, and this is the reason why, when we meet with him at all before this period, it is only in Asia; but here is a letter to his flock, and the letter, moreover, written by an Apostle; we shall certainly therein find some mention of him. Paul, who loves to salute in detail all those whom he addresses, must of necessity treat of such questions as most nearly concern them, and were it on no other ground than the love or respect which he would naturally bear to his colleague, or a proper regard for his prince or superior, he will at least salute him: at all events, he cannot fail to make some allusion, however slight, either to his presence or to his long and past labours in this city. What is the fact? There is not a word—there is an absolute silence concerning St. Peter. Neither St. Paul seems to have thought of St. Peter, nor would the reader, in reading his epistle, dream of his existence. Nevertheless, St. Paul is profuse in salutations, occupies a whole chapter in nothing else, and salutes a multitude of persons employed in the Church. If we should say that St. Peter was absent we cannot escape the difficulty; for not only does Paul abstain from saluting Peter, but he writes positively to this flock as to a flock which had never yet seen an Apostle. 'I am ready,' he says, 'to preach the Gospel to you that are at Rome also' (i. 15), *i. e.* to preach the Gospel to the Christians of Rome—the flock of another, and that other the Prince of Apostles, established as their Bishop for some years. It is well known that St. Paul preferred to preach the Gospel where no other Apostle had preceded him; and, nevertheless, he sends to the Christians of this city exhortations and rules (xvi. 17); he desires to communicate to them some spiritual gift (i. 11), he praises them, he instructs them, he encourages them by name, and yet, in all this, not one word is to be found which can be construed into a reference to any residence, present or past, of St. Peter in this city. What would any bishop say to a priest, or even to a colleague, who should write in this manner to a flock over which he had presided for seventeen years? Doubtless, if such an one should come to his assistance, with the respect due from one colleague to another, he would receive him with gratitude; but if, on the contrary, he should make no mention whatever of the bishop, reprove, instruct, correct his flock, as though he were not in existence, he might be naturally led to inquire, who he was, and to advise him to abstain from meddling with the duties of others. St. Paul salutes in this flock five distinct classes of those who, it is asserted, were under the special charge of St. Peter (xvi. 5, 10, 11, 14, 15), and by name twenty-six different persons, several of whom he designated as 'his helpers in Christ' * (xvi. 3, 9) ;"—and not a word of St. Peter!

Roman Catholic writers, as, for instance, Baronius, Noel Alexandre, &c., vainly endeavour to

---

* A. Bost.

account for this forgetfulness, this omission, at once so remarkable and humiliating. It is difficult to decide whether they speak seriously, or whether they abuse their influence over weak minds, when they seek to have it believed that the reason why St. Paul presents no salutation to St. Peter, is simply because he was aware of the accidental absence of that bishop. Supposing this to have been this case, it would not weaken the powerful reasoning of this remarkable passage from the work of M. Bost. Moreover, these learned Papists assert, that if St. Paul, in writing to the Romans, does not salute St. Peter, neither, in writing to the Ephesians, does he salute Timothy, who, according to them, was at Ephesus when he wrote, neither, in his Epistle to the Hebrews, does he allude to the presence of St. James at Jerusalem.

Before we examine these objections with attention, we might, in all honesty and good faith, inquire, what must be the artificial and groundless nature of that system, which requires for its maintenance such pitiful subterfuges—such sorry expedients, in the explanation of a fact, which, if disproved, would alienate ninety-nine out of every hundred from their misplaced faith; but since it is antagonism, and not meditation, which these objections here require, we would simply ask these writers, where have you learned that St. Paul was informed of the absence of St. Peter ?— whence is it that you derive your proofs ? As to the assertion concerning Timothy and St. James, it seems to us quite sufficient to remark, in order to invalidate them, that,—

1. At the time when St. Paul wrote his Epistles to the Ephesians, to the Colossians, and to the Philippians, Timothy was at Rome; for these three Epistles were written during the residence of St. Paul at Rome (61-63), and the two last bear the inscription, "Paul and Timothy."

2. That the Epistle to the Hebrews does not contain, like that to the Romans, special references; and that to the Ephesians has no salutations.

3. That the Epistle to the Hebrews is not addressed exclusively to the Jews at Jerusalem, but to all converted Jews in all places, and that, consequently, there was no greater reason why St. James should be mentioned more than any other Apostle.

We are compelled, therefore, to conclude that

St. Paul knew not of the presence of St. Peter at Rome in the year 58.

Paul arrived himself in this city, and, as is well known, dwelt there in captivity from the year 61 to 63. St. Luke gives us not only the details of his voyage (Acts, xxvii. xxviii.), but also of his arrival and residence. Yet in the whole of this recital we do not find a word concerning the principal person of the Christian world—we do not find a word concerning St. Peter.*

Three days after his arrival Paul called the chief of the Jews together, and, as St. Luke relates (xxviii. 17, 18), set before them the causes of his presence in their midst. "And they said unto him, We neither received letters out of Judea concerning thee, neither any of the brethren who came shewed or spake any harm of thee. But we desire to hear of thee what thou thinkest: for as concerning this sect, we know that every where it

* A very curious excuse is offered by the Père Molkenbuhr, Provincial of the Recollets of theprovince of Lower Saxony, and Doctor of Divinity of the University of Heidelberg : " St. Luke wrote *to* Rome, and *for* the Romans. It is then natural that he should only recount to them that which they did not know."—*Binæ Dissertationes de Cathedra Romana et Antiochena.* 1788.

is spoken against. And when they had appointed him a day, there came many to him into his lodging; to whom he expounded and testified the kingdom of God, persuading them concerning Jesus, both out of the law of Moses and out of the Prophets, from morning till evening" (vv. 21-23).

It is clear from this that the great Apostle of the circumcision had not yet laboured amongst the Jews of the capital, since the chief amongst them were utterly ignorant of the elementary doctrines of Christianity. As for the Christian community of Rome, composed for the most part of heathen proselytes, a hasty reading of the epistles of Paul, and especially of that to the Romans, will suffice to shew which of the two Apostles, Peter or Paul, first entered into connexion with them, and justly merits the title of their spiritual guide.

Paul resided at Rome for two years, and freely preached the Gospel in that city; but he by no means forgot those whom he had already won to the faith in Greece and in Asia. It was during this period that he wrote his Epistles to the Philippians, to the Colossians, to the Ephesians, to Philemon, and, as is supposed, to the Hebrews.

A perusal of these Epistles gives us a complete

and clear idea of the condition of the Roman Church; but in spite of all the details we meet with, we shall not be able to find the least trace of an episcopate at Rome, of a settled ecclesiastical organisation, and much less of St. Peter.

In these Epistles we see the great and illustrious missionary to the Gentiles the object of continual attacks from those Judaising Christians, who proclaimed the observance of the ceremonial law to be a necessary condition of admission into the bosom of the Church : we admire his ardour and his faith, and we rejoice in his triumph. How was it, however, that Peter, at that time president of the Christian community for twenty-three years, had not better succeeded in dissipating those very prejudices which the Council at Jerusalem had so vigorously combated? Was it that he had fallen from his lightning-like ardour into indolence and discouragement? Had he, a second time faithless, abandoned the pure and holy cause of the Gospel? Can we dare to believe it? We cannot, for his Epistles prove the contrary.

Paul found himself in want at Rome. Who at that time furnished him with the means of subsistence? Not the Christians at Rome, for they had not yet amassed the riches of the four quarters of the globe. It was from the city of Philippi that help came to him. History does not speak of any eagerness on the part of the Romans to aid him. It is not likely, however, to suppose that they had abandoned him. We dare not suggest that St. Peter could have neglected his needy brother; and we are therefore forced to conclude that no Church of such a standing as is asserted existed at Rome, and that St. Peter was not present as its bishop.

But there is yet another supposition. Perhaps Paul, through some movement of pride, or some coolness towards him whom he had formerly blamed at Antioch, did not choose to recognise the Bishop of Rome, and thus passed over in silence all that related to his labours, to his disciples, and to his success, despising the Christian episcopate established at Rome for so many years. If the Spirit poured forth on the day of Pentecost, and that by which Paul was animated in his persecuting journey to Damascus, had borne similar fruits, we then should have good reason to avoid and mistrust an edifice which, in its very foundation, should be so defiled.

In reading the passages in Colossians (iv. 10–14), Philemon (23, 24), we find St. Paul naming his friends, his fellow-labourers, his comforters, whilst St. Peter, the chief disciple of Christ, the primate of the Church, is not even mentioned. This silence is inexplicable.

The learned and skilful champions of the pontifical throne suppose that he was again on some journey of inspection. But this does not touch the question; for we have proved not only that he was not *at that time* at Rome, but that he never had been. On what ground, moreover, is it that these frequent excursions, even as far as England, are asserted? There are no proofs existent drawn from any source. Something more than mere hypothesis is needed for the submission of the conscience and the bending of the knee to the sovereign pontiff of Rome.

We see no proof whatever of any presence of St. Peter at Rome before the year 63.

It is not known with any degree of certitude where St. Paul directed his steps immediately after his release from his captivity at Rome, whether or not he then realised the intention expressed in Romans xv. 24, of taking a journey into Spain. As, however, according to Pagi, there only remained to him two years, or, according to other defenders of the Romanist tradition (who place the period of his death in the year 67), four years to live, it is scarcely possible that he could in this space of time have visited the Spanish peninsula, equal in extent to that of Asia Minor, have again traversed Greece, Asia Minor, the island of Crete, and passed a whole winter at Nicopolis, a city of Epirus or Macedonia.

We are therefore led to believe that, having renounced his project of going into Spain, he went from Rome into Greece, according to his desire expressed in Philemon 22; Philippians, i. 25-26; ii. 24; and that he passed the last years of his life in these countries and in Asia Minor. The long journeys that the distance of the several places visited from each other necessitated, the lengthened residence which he made in the cities which he entered, constrain us to this supposition. We are therefore disposed to give credit to the general opinion, that St. Paul returned a second time to Rome, and suffered martyrdom in that city in the year 67. It was during this second residence at Rome, the duration of which is unknown, that he wrote his Second Epistle to Timothy, whom he had left at Ephesus. Nothing in this Epistle can lead us to suppose a residence of St. Peter in the place from whence it is dated.

On the contrary, there are passages, such, for instance, as the following, which lead us strongly to believe that Rome was not yet the episcopate of St. Peter.

In the Second Epistle to Timothy, which was the last that St. Paul wrote, for it was written in the prospect of his approaching death (iv. 6, 8), the Apostle beseeches Timothy to come to him (ver. 9); "for Demas," says he, "has forsaken me, having loved this present world, and is departed unto Thessalonica, Crescens to Galatia, Titus unto Dalmatia; ONLY *Luke is with me*. Take Mark, and bring him with thee; for he is profitable to me for the ministry. And Tychicus have I sent to Ephesus" (10–12). "At my first answer NO MAN stood with me, but ALL MEN forsook me: I pray God that it may not be laid to their charge" (16). "Eubulus greeteth thee, and Pudens, and Linus, and Claudia, and all the brethren" (21).

We might reasonably have expected that in such an Epistle, and under such circumstances, some mention would have been made of St. Peter had he been at this time either present in, or Bishop of, Rome. It is difficult to believe that in the very place where these words were written there could have been a Church founded, sustained, and guided by such an Apostle as St. Peter.

To admit at such a time the Roman episcopate of St. Peter is indeed an insult to his memory; and the puerile excuse that the bishop was again absent on some journey has more the character of a bad jest than a grave effort for the maintenance of the Romish primacy, or of St. Peter's supremacy.

Tillemont seeks to exculpate St. Peter (whom he certainly must have had in his mind, though he does not specially name him, because the presence of St. Peter at Rome was never to him a matter of doubt) in this reasoning. He says, "This crime (that of abandoning St. Paul) can only be charged upon those who, having some credit at the court, could have aided him if they had manifested the courage which they ought to have shewn; it cannot be charged upon St. Luke and the other saints who were then at Rome, and who possessed, without doubt, sufficient courage and generosity to expose their life for him, but who would only have done so uselessly, being not less guilty than himself in the estimation of the persecutors."*—*Mémoires*, i. p. 689. Now

* The explanation of Tillemont does not invalidate the author's reasoning. The question is whether St. Peter was at

there is no reference whatever in the complaint of St. Paul to any interference on his behalf to the authorities; he speaks simply of *abandonment*— of that consolation which Onesiphorus afforded him, and which they left him to need. "The Lord give mercy unto the house of Onesiphorus," says the Apostle, "for he oft refreshed me (ἀνέψυξε), and was not *ashamed of my chain*; but when he was at Rome he sought me out very diligently, and found me."

Neither St. Luke nor St. Paul say one word concerning a Roman bishop, or of St. Peter as that bishop: it remains for us to consult his own Epistles. It is natural to suppose that he will in them give evidence of his own eminent position, in order to leave the remembrance of it to future generations.

We cannot, however, undertake the examination of these two Epistles without being first struck with the reflection, that of the gigantic energy

that time present in, or Bishop of Rome? The assertion is, that there is no mention or allusion to him whatever; that, moreover, it is not probable that he would have abandoned St. Paul in his extremity. We know Luke was at Rome, for he is named; but the reasoning which would exculpate him proves nothing with regard to St. Peter, of whose existence at Rome at this time there is not the slightest trace."—TRANSLATOR.

attributed to the primate of the Christian Church, only two small Epistles, written to the Churches of the East, should have reached us as the fruit. It is remarkable that there is not a single letter of exhortation or of consolation to that beloved Church at Rome, from which his Apostolic functions so often separated him, and of which he was the head for a period of twenty-five years.

Now in opening these two Epistles we do not find a single word of Rome, not the least allusion to his pre-eminence, to his exalted position, or to his particular mission. On the contrary, in his truly Christian humility — and it is indeed in this that he is eminently distinguished from his pretended successors—he names the faithful, to whom he writes, "lively stones built up a spiritual house," and designates the elders of the Church not as sons or subordinates, but as colleagues, as *co-priests*, speaking of himself as συμπρεσβυτερος (1 Pet. v. 1).

At length, towards the close of this Epistle, arises out of this desolate sea, out of this vast blank, a solid and tangible ground for the support of the Romish assumption. Babylon, of which mention is made, must certainly mean Rome: this cannot be contradicted. Peter, anxious to conceal under this false name and much-used metaphor the real place of his residence, uses it in order to avoid (*i. e.* after a period of twenty-five years had elapsed) the consequences of his escape from prison at Jerusalem, and in order to preserve the Church of Rome from the persecution of the heathen authorities.*

This last foundation must perish, like the rest; for, in the first place, it was not in the nature or character of St. Peter to fear the consequences of an honest truth; he never used an artifice to avoid them. In the second place, this letter, confided to the care of Silvanus (who was, in all probability, the same person as Silas the companion of St. Paul), was not likely to have fallen into the hands of the heathens, he being himself the bearer of it. In the third place, when there is not sufficient reason for torturing a word in order to extract its true meaning, we prefer to keep to the literal sense. Peter was the Apostle of the dispersed Jews ; nothing, therefore, was more natural than that he should have come to Babylon. Now by this name not only were the ruins of ancient Babylon designated, but the new city of Seleucia, constructed

* Vide Natalis Alexander, "Dissertat." p. 168, col. 2,

by Seleucus-Nicator 297 years before Christ, and situated on the Tigris at about thirteen leagues distance from the ancient Babylon.*

M. Ellendorf, as well as other commentators, lays great stress upon the *order* of the inscription of the first Epistle, "to the strangers scattered throughout Pontus, Galatia, Cappadocia, Asia, and Bithynia:" he judges from this that St. Peter wrote from some place geographically nearer to Pontus than to Bithynia.

Lastly, the mention made of the Epistles of St. Paul, "our beloved brother Paul," (2 Pet. iii. 15), and the evil interpretations to which they had given rise, lead us to believe that St. Peter had been a witness rather to the effect which these letters had produced, than to their actual reception either at Rome or elsewhere.

Peter himself gives us, then, no aid whatever

---

* Vide Joseph. "Antiq." xv. 2, 2, xvii. 2, 1, where mention is made of the real Babylon and of a Jewish community which existed there. Vide, also, as to the false interpretation of this word Babylon, introduced into the Church by Papias, Pearson, "Opera Posthuma Chronologica," Lond. 1688, p. 56; Tillemont, "Mém." I. note xxxi. p. 748; Andrew Blanc, "On the Primacy of the Pope and the Abode of St. Peter at Rome," (Paris, 1838), p. 33; and lastly, the article "Peter" in the Encyclopedia of Ersch et Gruber, 3d sect. 19th part, p. 357.

in the discovery of any trace that might justify the pomp and splendour with which the Romish Church has thought proper to surround this Apostle.

Our examination of the Scriptures is now finished. We gather from it definitively the following results:—

1. That the conversion of St. Paul, not taking place before the year 39, for the reasons given, it was not till towards the year 42 that Paul went to Jerusalem in order to visit Peter, who at that time was there.

2. That shortly after the departure of St. Paul for Tarsus, Peter visited the different Churches of Palestine.

3. That during a mission of the Apostles Paul and Barnabas to Jerusalem, Peter was there imprisoned by order of Herod, the fourth year of the reign of Claudius, or the year of Christ 45.

4. That in accordance with the special vocation of St. Peter, it is possible that after his deliverance from prison this Apostle went into the East, in order to preach the Gospel, and that we cannot discover the least datum which leads us to believe in a journey into the West.

5. That Peter assisted at the council of Jeru-

BOOKS OF THE NEW TESTAMENT. 73

salem, and that, as far as can be gathered from the recital of St. Luke, without any character of pre-eminence or presidency.

(According to Baronius, this council took place in 48; according to Noël Alexandre, in 51; and according to others, whom we have followed, in 52 or 53.)

6. That after this he went to Antioch, and from thence probably into the East.

7. That the Epistle of St. Paul to the Romans, written in 58, makes no mention whatever of any residence of St. Peter at Rome, either present or past.

8. That the silence concerning St. Peter in the recital of St. Luke (Acts xxviii.), and in the Epistles to the Christians of Philippi, of Colosse, to the Hebrews, and to Philemon, all written at Rome between the years 61 and 63, make it evident that up to that time Peter personally was a stranger to the Romans.

9. That the second Epistle to Timothy, written at Rome a little while before the death of St. Paul, says nothing concerning St. Peter, and thus invalidates the tradition of a contemporaneous death of these two Apostles.

10. Lastly, that the writings of St. Peter

himself do not contain the slightest allusion to Rome, and that other circumstances referred to in them strengthen the opinion that the seat of his labour was the East, and that the sense bestowed upon the word Babylon is arbitrary, forced, and without warrant.

PETER NEVER DWELT AT ROME, or, if he did, it was not till the period of his death. The Bible declares it plainly for him who is willing to read. He could not therefore in that place found a church, preside over it, nor transmit the government of it to a successor. The sacred writers, animated with that spirit of truth which Christ the Lord their Master bequeathed unto them, would not have concealed a fact from us upon which the spiritual existence of all the faithful was to depend. Would not the evidence of St. Luke, St. Paul, St. James, St. John, St. Peter himself, have far outweighed the assertions of a small number of writers, who are, after all, but men under the influence of passion, of errors, and of pious delusions, who contradict and confute each other in all which they assert, and decline for themselves the privilege of infallibility? The silence of the Apostles is in itself a witness which cannot be gainsaid by the mere assertion of men interested in the maintenance of a system which has no scriptural foundation.

The Bible contradicts the tradition of Rome; intelligence and good sense revolt against it; history overthrows it: and yet this tradition still exists in all the impregnable grandeur to which the ambition of a sect has raised it. Still it triumphs over all the texts of that Scripture whose divine character the Romish Church herself has never dared to attack. Be it so. This Medusa head of heresy, that thus comes in between the faithful and eternal light, shall one day perish and be trodden under foot by the truthful force of history.

Let us not, however, be wanting to the memory of those learned writers who have *honestly* yielded their faith and lent their aid to this tradition: to them be all honour and respect. We would not charge upon them the deplorable effects of their ignorance or infirmity. They little dreamed that the day would come when they should be constituted the tyrants of the human mind, or that their errors would leave such deep traces. They were themselves humble men; and without this humility, which sits so well alike on the modest disciple and the learned doctor, they never would have written the passages that follow —passages that make it clearly manifest how great a value they set on that authority which until now we have invoked.

"The Scriptures are perfect, for they are the words of God, which His Spirit has dictated, and they *alone* make up that Apostolic tradition manifested to the whole world, and which the Church addresses plainly to whomsoever will hear the truth."—IRENÆUS, *Adv. Hæres.* ii. 47 ; iii. 2.

"I adore the fulness of the Scriptures, I admit nothing without their witness. Let him, then, who produces aught than that which is written fear that word 'woe' pronounced against the man who adds to the Scripture; for to know nothing but that, as Theophylactus says, is to know all things."—TERTULLIAN, *Contra Hermog.*; THEOPHYLACTUS, *in Epist. ad Gal.* c. 1.

"From whence comes this pretended tradition? God declares that we must do that *which is written.*"—CYPRIAN, Epist. lxxiv.

"How diabolical is the thought that there can be any right teaching apart from the holy and sovereign Scriptures!"— THEOPHILUS of Alexandria, *in Epist. Pasch.*

"It is the oracles of God which bring forth

for us the true rule of the true faith, and of all truth."—CHRYSOSTOM, *Serm. XI. de Sanct. Pentec.*

"It is a criminal pride to add to the Scripture that *which is not written.*"—BASIL, *Liber de Confess. Fidei.*

"Let us compare all discourses and writings with the doctrines of the Bible, and let us only accept those which are conformed to the Scriptures."—BASIL, *In Ascet. Def.* 72.

"Do not tell me," says Augustine, "of the authority of this or that council: it is to that of the canonical books, and to none other, that I submit."—AUG. *De Doct. Christ.* &c.

"The things that we invent ourselves," says St. Jerome (*Ad. 1 c. in Aggæi.*), "and pass off as Apostolical traditions, without the authority and testimony of holy Scripture, must be stricken with the sword of God."

"By the holy Scriptures alone am I persuaded," says Theodoret, *Dialog.* 1.

We might easily multiply such passages, but these will suffice; we will only add that which a celebrated Romish theologian recalled to the recollection of the Council of Constance:—

"The infallible Church is neither that of Africa, that of Rome, nor a representative Church assembling in a council, for councils have often erred; but it is the Church of Jesus Christ, extended throughout all the earth, and she is this Church, because that in her are to be found the Holy Scriptures."—TH. NETTER. *Doct. Fidei,* ii. 2, 19.

(The works of this theologian were approved by a bull of Pope Martin V.—BASNAGE, xxvii. 3.)

Popes and Councils! burn as you will the Bibles which you find in the cottages of the poor, never will you be able to exterminate the spirit of truth which springs from so pure a source. The day shall come when that truth shall overthrow your power, as the inspired shepherd of Israel, in the simplicity and strength of his faith, cast the gigantic Philistine to the ground.

CHAPTER III.

EXAMINATION OF THE TRADITION.

AFTER having, in the preceding chapter, appealed to the authority of the canonical books of the New Testament, and demonstrated, at its close, the weight attributed to that authority, even by those who compose in themselves the formidable power called *tradition*, we will now proceed to the refutation of the passages which the Romish Church has drawn from this very tradition for the support of her system, and for the laying the foundation of a *cathedra Petri* — a chair really occupied by St. Peter. We hope to bring to light the corrupt elements which have been introduced into this tradition, for some of which the writers themselves, blinded by interest or religious fanaticism, are responsible, and the rest of which must be attributed to the general character of the primitive ages of the Church.

It is not our intention to deal with any other writings than those which have been established by a just criticism as authentic, or which, at least, are generally accounted to possess some historical value. We shall have occasion, ere we close the subject, to say all that is necessary concerning the apocryphal writings, which are the true source of the historical legends concerning St. Peter.

Clement of Rome, the third bishop of this city, and a contemporary of the Apostles Peter and Paul, thus writes to the Corinthians, in the fifth chapter of his first Epistle:—

"Let us set before our eyes the holy Apostles: Peter, by unjust envy, underwent, not one or two, but many sufferings; till at last, being martyred, he went to the place of glory that was due unto him. For the same cause did Paul, in like manner, receive the reward of his patience. Seven times he was in bonds; he was whipped, was stoned; he preached both in the East and in the West, leaving behind him the glorious report of his faith; and so, having taught the whole world righteousness, and for that end travelled even to the utmost bounds of the West, he at last suffered martyrdom by the command of the governors, and departed out of the world and went unto his holy place, being become a most eminent pattern of patience unto all ages."

This passage suggests to us the following remarks:—

1. That there is not here the least mention of a bishoprick of St. Peter at Rome.

2. That Clement, the asserted successor of St. Peter, might very legitimately and with good reason have enlarged somewhat more on the Apostolic activity of his predecessor, more, at any rate, than he has done on the labours and sufferings of St. Paul.

3. That Clement, from his manner of speaking, leads us to the conclusion, contrary to the common opinion, that the death of Paul was subsequent to that of Peter.

4. That this passage proves clearly, like many others, that no distinction of rank existed between the two great Apostles.

5. That this twofold mention of the extension of the evangelical labours of the Apostle Paul, even to the limits of the West—a mention which breathes the gratitude of the writer who had

gathered the fruits of these labours — is here made as constituting a special title of glorification and merit to the Apostle Paul alone.

St. Ignatius (bishop of Antioch, who suffered martyrdom at Rome under the reign of Trajan in the earlier years of the second century) would have had more than all others powerful motives for speaking of St. Peter, writing as he did from Antioch, where that Apostle ministered as bishop for the space of seven years according to tradition, to the Christians of Rome, where the same Apostle held a bishoprick for twenty-five years, and where, to this day, his tomb is professedly shewn. Yet there is not in his epistle a word concerning these traditional facts. The silence is astonishing: it is simply said, "Pray, therefore, unto Christ for me, that by these instruments I may be made the sacrifice of God. I do not, as Peter and Paul, command you: they were Apostles, I a condemned man; they were free, but I am even to this day a servant."

These words, worthy of such a bishop as Ignatius, far from supporting the pretensions of the Romish Church, prove on the contrary the co-ordination of the two principal Apostles, and the great distance which the Bishop of Antioch considered to exist between a weak bishop and the immediate disciples of Christ.

Supposing even that the mention of Peter's name ought properly to lead to the inference, as it has done, that he was known to the Romans, who will assure us that the word *Petrus* has not been interpolated by some copyist? For all critics are agreed as to the many forgeries of the text of the epistles of Ignatius.*

But the same epistle of which we speak presents another circumstance which is worthy of a special notice. The inscription which it bears, and which will be here transcribed, makes it sufficiently evident that the writer by no means considered the Church which he addressed as the principal of the Christian congregations, and that he, at least, did not recognise in the capital of the Empire, the pretended metropolis of Christianity, either the existence of any bishop or chief as the successor of St. Peter, or of any sovereign master in the affairs of religion.

Of the two inscriptions which are extant, that which the learned Usserius has approved, and

---

* Vide Pearson, " Vindic. Ignat." ch. vi. p. 270; Le Clerc, " Biblioth. Ancienne et Moderne," tom. xix. p. 388; Guillon, " Biblioth. Choisie des Pères" (edit. Louvain), tom. i. p. 127.

which is contained in the Acts of the Martyrdom of Ignatius related by Simeon Metaphrastes, is chosen. It commends itself by its brevity and simplicity, when compared with the tissue of eulogies, badly conceived, which the ordinary text presents, and which is evidently the work of some professional interpolator. "Ignatius, surnamed Theophorus, bishop of the holy Church at Antioch, to the Church which has obtained mercy through the greatness of the Almighty Father and the Lord Jesus Christ, his only Son, sanctified and enlightened by the will of Him who hath willed all things which belong to the faith and grace of Jesus Christ our God and Saviour; to her who holds the chief rank in the place of the country of the Romans" (ἥτις καὶ προκάθηται ἐν τόπῳ χωρίου Ῥωμαίων*). This passage certainly speaks of a pre-eminence, of a distinction which this Christian congregation enjoyed amongst the Romans generally, but not of any superiority over

---

* "Ignatius, qui et Theophorus .... misericordiam consecutæ in magnificentiâ altissimi Dei Patris et Jesu Christi, unigeniti Filii, ecclesiæ, sanctificatæ et illuminatæ per voluntatem Dei operati omnia quæ pertinent ad fidem et charitatem Jesu Christi Dei et Salvatoris nostri, quæ præsidet *in loco Romanæ regionis,*" &c.—*Sacræ Biblioth. Vet. Patrum,* Paris, 1610.

any other Christian Church. It is but another form, and the confirmation, in some respects, of that eulogy which St. Paul had already given to these very Romans in the Epistle which he addressed to them in the year 58. (Romans, i. 8.) If we compare this inscription with those of the epistle to the Ephesians and Smyrnæans, we shall be convinced that it contains nothing upon which the Romans may especially vaunt over others. "At all events," says a commentator upon the Epistles of Ignatius,[*] " the first remark that naturally presents itself in the perusal of these words is, that Ignatius addresses his letter simply to the *Church at Rome*, not to the Pope, not to the holy Father, not to the Pastor of the universal Church, not to the Vicar of Jesus, neither to the holy Apostolic See, nor to the holy College of Cardinals. These titles were then unknown, or, if known, were given equally and indifferently to all bishops and their sees. St. Ignatius does not even address his letter, as it would seem he should have done, to the *Bishop of Rome*, since there must have been one at that time. Where,

[*] Abr. Ruchat. " Lettres et Monuments de Trois Pères Apostoliques, St. Clément de Rome, St. Ignace d'Antioche, et St. Polycarpe de Smyrne," Leyde, 1738, tom. i. p. 177.

then, was this pretended centre of unity, concerning which men now talk so loudly, and which, like Medusa's head, stupifies so many? St. Ignatius knew it not."

Justin Martyr, about 150 years after Christ.

Nothing can be found in the writings of this celebrated apologist for Christianity which will lead us to believe in the fact so categorically established by the Romish Church. It is true he recounts the journey of Simon the Sorcerer to Rome, his abode in that city, and the miracles which he is said to have wrought; he relates, moreover, that the Romans, accounting him a God, had erected a statue to his honour, which he himself had seen.* But he says not a word of him who, according to the tradition, had triumphed over this impostor, and who had

* The statue of a Sabine god, bearing the inscription SANCTO SANCO SEMONI DEO FIDIO, as related by Gruber ("Thesaur. Inscript." p. xcvi. n. 6), has given rise to the story of the honours decreed by the Romans to this celebrated magician.—Vide VALESIUS *ad Euseb.* ii. 13; PETAVIUS *in Hæres. Menandr.* n. 5.

Concerning Simon himself consult the notes of Tillemont ("Mémoires," edit. de Brux. tom. iii. p. 346); Moreri's "Historical Dictionary," under the word "Papias;" St. Augustine, Ep. lxxxvi. *ad Cos.*

undertaken a journey to Rome for the very purpose of destroying his pernicious influence. It may fairly be concluded from this that the story of Simon, originating in an evident mistake, had not in the time of Justin acquired that importance and credibility which were subsequently given to it. At all events, we can gather clearly from Justin Martyr's account that he was completely ignorant of the purpose generally attributed to St. Peter in undertaking this journey to Rome, even if he were aware of any residence of the Apostle in that city.

The order of chronological inquiry at length brings us to him who may fairly be considered as the author of this legend, and who by his forgeries, wilful or innocent, has led all the writers who have followed him into error; thus laying, though perhaps unconsciously, the foundations of that powerful system which, by its ideal grandeur and material force, has alike subjugated, during a series of ages, the mighty and the feeble of Christendom. We allude to Papias, bishop of Hierapolis in Phrygia. It is on the assertions of this saint that Eusebius affirms the journey of St. Peter; and it is on the authority of the latter that the Romish Church bases her claim to the successorship of the Apostle.

Papias was, as Jerome informs us (Epist. xxix.), the instructor of Irenæus, and lived, according to Eusebius, in the third generation following the Apostles.* This last circumstance is of the greatest consequence to our argument, for it proves, in explicit terms, that the first and second generation after the Apostles had not dared to advance any thing concerning the pretended see of St. Peter at Rome. Papias is the *first* who reveals this fact to us; but, unfortunately for those who place faith in him, not only are his intellectual capacities contested, but he is charged with a fault which must deeply compromise him with every Christian man,—and that is neither more nor less than a want of honesty. Here is the testimony of Eusebius: "Papias was of a limited intelligence (*mediocri admodum ingenio præditus*), as his writings prove; he has left

---

* Irenæus adv. Hæres. v. 33: "*Iste Papias Joannis auditor, Polycarpi familiaris, vir antiquus.*" This John is not the Apostle, but the elder of that name. Vide St. Jerome in Catalogo et Baronius *ad an.* 118. Papias is said to be the author of the five books "De Interpretatione Oraculorum Dominicorum."

behind him several things which bear too much of the character of the fabulous; and he has even furnished to several ecclesiastical writers after him the means of falling into error in alleging the antiquity of this witness." The Bishop of Cæsarea quotes, as instances amongst others, his opinion on the thousand years' reign of Jesus Christ (III. 33), and his fabrications concerning the daughters of the Apostle Philip, as having retained their virginity, and surviving to his time.* All this shews no very brilliant testimony in his favour on the part of Eusebius, and tends to prove that the declaration made by the same writer elsewhere, and in an opposite sense, is an interpolation not to be found in ancient manuscripts, as H. Valois assures us.†

Let us now examine the passages of Papias, from which, according to the Romish writers, results the incontestable proof of St. Peter's

* The invention rests upon an exaggeration of the fact contained in Acts, xxi. 9, where mention is made of the four daughters of Philip the Evangelist, one of the seven deacons, who were virgins, and prophesied. Notwithstanding the absurdity of the fable invented by Papias, it was repeated by Clement of Alexandria and Polycrates of Ephesus.

† Tom. III. c. 30. "Vir imprimis disertus et eruditus, an Scripturarum peritus."

bishoprick at Rome. They are extracted from Eusebius, for we have only a few scattered remnants of this Father's writings extant.

"Tantus autem veritatis fulgor emicuit in mentibus eorum, qui Petrum audierant, *ut parum habentes semel audiisse*, sed Marcum, Petri sectatorem, cujus hodie exstat evangelium, enixe rogarent ut doctrinæ illius scriptum monumentum apud se relinqueret. Nec prius destiterunt, quam hominem *expugnassent*, auctoresque scribendi illius quod secundum Marcum dicitur evangelii exstitissent. Quod quum Petrus *revelatione S. Spiritus* cognovisset, librum illum auctoritate sua comprobasse dicitur, ut deinceps in ecclesia legeretur. Refertur id a Clemente in VI. libro Institutionum, cui testis etiam accedit Papias, Hierapolis episcopus. Porro Marci mentionem fieri aiunt a Petro in priori epistola quam Romæ scriptam contendunt, idque ipsum Petrum innuere qui figurate Romam Babylonem appellat, his verbis . . . . . " — EUSEB. *Hist. Eccles.* ii. 14.

"Aiebat," says Papias, "presbyter ille Joannes, Marcum Petri interpretem quæcumque memoriæ mandaverat, diligenter perscripsisse, non tamen ordine pertexuisse, quæ a Domino aut dicta aut gesta fuerant. Neque enim ipse Dominum audiverat, neque sectatus fuerat unquam, sed cum Petro postea versatus est, qui pro audientium utilitate, non vero ut sermonum Domini historiam contexeret, evangelium prædicabat." — EUSEB. *Hist. Eccles.* iii. 38.

As may be seen, the first passage does not literally belong to Papias; but direct reference is made to his testimony. In either case the whole account is too fabulous, as M. Ellendorf has justly observed, for it stands thus. Peter had been for several years Bishop of Rome; the Romans notwithstanding addressed themselves to Mark, in order to induce him to commit to writing the teaching of Peter, lest they should forget that which they had only *once* heard. Moreover, Mark complied with this request at the suggestion of St. Peter, who only knew of their wish by the inspiration of the Holy Ghost. St. Peter, in his second Epistle to the Jews of Pontus, &c., thus writes (2 Pet. i. 15), "Moreover I will endeavour, that ye may be able after my decease to have these things always in remembrance. For we have not followed cunningly devised fables, when we made known unto you the power and coming of our Lord Jesus Christ, but were eye-witnesses of His majesty." From this it would seem that if there were any design of reducing the evangelical teaching of the Apostle to writing, he would have undertaken it himself rather than have left it to Mark.

The second passage, extracted literally from Papias, who himself founds it on the authority of the Elder John, proves still more the truth of the evidence of Eusebius concerning him, "that he was equally wanting in sagacity as credibility," for it will be sufficient to remember,

1. That Mark wrote his Gospel in *Greek*, and not in *Latin*, as the purpose attributed to him would lead us to infer.*

2. That the Romish Church herself affirms that he was Bishop of Alexandria.

3. That the companion and spiritual son of St. Peter composed his Gospel, according to Irenæus, after the death of St. Peter and St. Paul.

The authority of this *vir antiquus*, so very

* Vide "Biographie Universelle," under the word "Marc," and Tillemont, "Mémoires," édit. de Brux. tom. ii. 1 partie, p. 393.

generally invoked, thus becomes reduced, in effect, to little better than nothing.

The passage of Eusebius, which we have just quoted on the subject of Papias, appeals also to the authority of Clement, of Alexandria, who perfectly agrees with Papias in what he says touching the Gospel by St. Mark. Nevertheless, in the citation of the words of Clement, extracted by Eusebius from the "Recognitiones" of this Father,* a slight discrepancy is observable. It is there said that St. Peter neither consented to nor opposed the project of St. Mark (μήτε κωλῦσαι μήτε προτρέψασθαι). Clement, who lived towards the close of the second century, might well have drawn his statement, as Eusebius leads us to suppose, from the impure sources of Papias, and therefore merits no more confidence than that which is due to the Bishop of Hierapolis. But we have happily two arguments to adduce against the credibility of the assertions of Clement.

In the first place, we know that the historical criticisms of the famous doctor of Alexandria are very far from complete or probable, and we have

* Eusebius, "Hist. Eccl." vi. 11.

every right to place the assertion above quoted, concerning the Gospel of St. Mark, amongst such facts as Clement relates in the seven books of his "Stromata;" as for instance,—

1. That Christ preached but one year.

2. That the Apostle Matthias is identical with Zaccheus.

3. That St. Matthew never ate meat.

4. That Paul was married (Eusebius, iii. 24).

5. That Simon heard St. Peter preach after Marcion, who, nevertheless, did not live till the reign of Adrian or Antoninus.

6. That the Gospels *secundum Hebræos et Ægyptios* are not apocryphal.

7. That St. Peter is the author of an Apocalypse and Discourse, passages of which he quotes.

In spite of the splendid testimonies which are given in his favour by Eusebius, Cyril, and Photius (vide Tillemont, "Mémoires," iii. p. 195), we are firmly of opinion, that Clement of Alexandria was after all a very sorry historian. But as to the passage immediately before us *he is not responsible for it;* for it has been proved that the "Recognitiones," attributed to him by Eusebius, were never written by him, and this is the second

EXAMINATION OF THE TRADITION. 95

argument which we have to adduce in proof of the nullity of the fragment cited by Eusebius.

Hegesippus of Jerusalem, who died towards the year 180, certainly lived at Rome for the space of twenty years; but the very few fragments preserved by Eusebius, of a work of five volumes, and which, according to this historian,* embraced the whole history of the Church, from the death of our Lord until the times of the author, teach us nothing concerning any residence of St. Peter at Rome. The work entitled "De Excidio Hierosolymæ," which mentions this fact, is evidently falsely attributed to Hegesippus, and was fabricated during the fourth century on the authority of some apocryphals, which then passed with the names of Linus and Marcellus. (This even Baronius and Labbé confess.) It is in this book that the fable of St. Peter's meeting with our Lord at the gates of Rome is found.

Denis of Corinth, who died about the year 178.

The testimony of this bishop, probably, offers the greatest difficulty of all others to those who deny the journey, in question, of St. Peter to Rome; for besides that he generally enjoys a

---

* Eusebius, iv. 8.

high reputation as an authority, he lived very close upon the Apostolic times, and his words are very clear and explicit on the subject. Amongst the few fragments of his writings found in Eusebius there is one which is thus expressed (ii. 24) : " The two Apostles St. Peter and Paul came into our city and instructed us, sowing the seed of evangelical doctrine; then afterwards they passed *at the same time* (together) into Italy, and after having instructed you in the same manner, they there suffered martyrdom."

Without being desirous in the least to write aught against the memory of the pious Bishop of Corinth, we will oppose to these words, decisive in appearance, the following considerations.

1. It is surprising that a Bishop of Corinth, towards the middle of the second century, should have asserted that St. Peter, with St. Paul, was the founder of the Church of Corinth. Could he then have been ignorant of the Epistles addressed by St. Paul to the Christians of that illustrious city, and which ought to have been in the possession of the Church, either in the original or copy? Now, in these Epistles, Paul clearly claims, without any participation by another, the honour of giving spiritual birth to the Christian

community at Corinth. He says, distinctly,—
"Though ye have ten thousand instructors in
Christ, yet have ye not many fathers, for in
Christ Jesus I have begotten you through the
Gospel" (1 Cor. iv. 15). He speaks in the same
sense, iii. 6-10, and ix. 1, 2.

2. The fact mentioned by Denis of the Apostolical labours of St. Peter at Corinth, is not verified by any other passage of sacred antiquity.* Moreover, in the supposition of the correctness of this fact, it would be inconceivable that Clement, the immediate successor of St. Peter at Rome, should have shewn so little interest in the teachings of his master at Corinth as not to allude to them at all in his Epistle to the Corinthians, which we have before mentioned, whilst in it he speaks so often of the labours and instructions of St. Paul.

3. St. Peter was never at Corinth, unless it were towards the year 65 or 66. For it was not until then that it could have been possible,—we say *possible*,—that Paul could have gone to Rome *passing by Corinth*. Every time that he had

* The passage in 1 Cor. i. 12, where mention is made of *Cephas*, in nowise proves the presence of St. Peter at Corinth; most theologians are agreed in this.

visited this city, he had quitted it in order to return to Asia (Acts, xviii. 18; xx. 1, and following): and in his first journey to Rome he did not pass by Corinth (Acts, xxvii. xxviii.). It could only have been possible,—and this is conceding a great deal when certain passages of Scripture, such as Titus, iii. 12, are considered—it could only have been possible that Paul, going for the last time into Italy, should have been joined by St. Peter at Corinth.

4. But this supposition will compel us to admit, that the Apostle St. Peter could not have visited the capital of the empire at this epoch (65 or 66), and this fact of itself utterly destroys the tradition of a twenty-five years' episcopate at Rome.

The words of St. Denis, whether they really belong to this bishop or not, are but a new proof of the tendency, so early manifested amongst the Christian Churches, to surround themselves with glory, in tracing their foundation to one or other of these two great missionary Apostles. Corinth, it would seem, was not exempt from the general and pious ambition.

We know that a multitude of errors, involuntary or wilful, unhappily prevailed and spread amongst the different churches from the first century, and that many apocryphal pieces were composed, either to establish heresies or to overthrow them. It may justly be said, without in the least compromising the dignity or truth of Christianity, that religious enthusiasm as well as blind fanaticism, that the efforts of the orthodox no less than the innovations of heretics, have thrown a thick veil over the ecclesiastical history of the earlier ages of the Church, and provoked doubts and mistrust even of the researches of Eusebius. The Bishop of Vence, Antoine Godeau, has frankly acknowledged, in the Preface to his Ecclesiastical History, that, from the Apostolical times down to the days of Pliny the younger, all was obscured and hidden in fables. Even what was written was not spared, and forgeries designedly made took place during the lifetime of the authors themselves. The same Denis, who has occasioned, in the consideration of his assertion, this observation, himself complains, in his letter to the Romans, that " the *ministers of the devil* (it is thus he qualifies heretics) had altered his letters, and filled them with their poison, in subtracting or adding just what pleased them ; but," he adds, " it is against them specially that this direful sentence has been pronounced: Woe unto you! After they have dared to corrupt the Holy Scriptures, it is not to be wondered at that they should not have treated writings of much less value with greater respect."*

The words of St. Denis of Corinth do not in any wise shake us in our opinion concerning the residence of St. Peter at Rome.

As to Irenæus, bishop of Lyons, who wrote some years after Denis, in the time of Eleutherius, bishop of Rome, about the year 180, we have already seen, in treating of Papias, to what his authority may be reduced. Eusebius has declared it in the passage already quoted: he is under the evil influence of Papias, his master, and, consequently, does not merit the historical confidence which is claimed for him. We possess, moreover, other assertions of his which compromise him as an historian of the Apostolical ages. Thus he pretends, in so many distinct terms, that our Lord was fifty years of age when he died, and asserts this on the authority of certain elders who had known St. John in Asia; and he thinks that

---

* Irenæus, p. 509, edition of Feu Ardent.

the reason of his living to that age was, that he might sanctify every period of human life. Another time he asserts, that Jesus was born in the forty-first year of the reign of Augustus, instead of the thirtieth, as the majority of authors affirm.

This doctor thus expresses himself on the foundation of ecclesiastical Rome: * " The blessed Apostles having founded and built up the Church of Rome, confided the ministry of the bishopric thereof to *Linus:* this is that Linus of whom St. Paul speaks in his Epistles to Timothy. Anacletus succeeded him. And Clement, who saw the blessed Apostles, and conferred with them, was the third from the Apostles after him who obtained the bishopric.

As to the mention of Linus in the Epistles of St. Paul, there is but one in 2 Timothy, iv. 21; and this passage, " Eubulus greeteth thee, and Pudens, and Linus, and Claudia," certainly does

* " Fundantes igitur et instruentes beati Apostoli (Petrus et Paulus) ecclesiam (Romæ) Lino episcopatum administrandæ ecclesiæ tradiderunt. Hujus Lini Paulus in his quæ sunt ad Timotheum epistolis meminit; succedit autem ei Anacletus: post eum tertio loco ab Apostolis episcopatum sortitur Clemens, qui et vidit ipsos Apostolos et contulit cum eis, cum adhuc insonantem prædicationem Apostolorum et traditionem ante oculos haberet."—*Adv. Hæres.* iii. 3.

not demonstrate that Linus possessed any distinction or authority.

Moreover, in the passage in question * we have only to deal with that which concerns the Apostles. Now, if there is any ground at all for admitting a foundation and hierarchical organisation of the Romish Church, there is much more ground for attributing the glory of this, if glory there be, to the Apostle St. Paul, if any faith is to be placed in the narrative of St. Luke and the Epistles of St. Paul.

Lastly (and here we have one of those numerous proofs of the uncertainty which characterises all traditions concerning ecclesiastical establishments and successions),† Tertullian, who wrote only

* In another place Irenæus affirms, that St. Matthew published his Gospel in Hebrew at the same time that Peter and Paul founded the Church at Rome. It is, therefore, undeniable, on the authority of Irenæus, that Paul is equally worthy of the glory with which, in later times, the name of Peter has been so exclusively and abundantly surrounded. The witness of Irenæus is repeated by Epiphanius. Irenæus says, (Ad. Hæres. l. iii. c. 3), "*Fundantes igitur et instruentes beati Apostoli* (Petrus et Paulus), *ecclesiam (Romanam),*" &c.

† "*Fluxa et dubia, quæ de summis pontificibus ad Victorem usque traduntur.*"—PETAVIUS, ii. 130.

"*Nec in tanta sæculorum caligine oculatissimi quique*

twenty years after Irenæus, declares (de Præscr. 32) that Peter had ordained Clement *first* Bishop of Rome, whilst that Irenæus counts him as *third*.

We will not trench here, although the passage of the Bishop of Lyons might legitimately lead us to do so, on another point of religious controversy, the corollary, in some sort, of our question, viz. whether Rome, as well as other Christian communities had or had not, during the Apostolic times, bishops in the later and modern acceptation of the word? The preceding remarks will suffice for rendering the assertions of Irenæus at least suspicious, and proving, that a very slight portion of credibility attaches to his testimony.

The testimonies quoted from Tertullian have no more consistency than the evidences which we have examined. Notwithstanding that, he tells us that *St. Peter was baptised in the Tiber* (de Baptismo, 4), and that *he was* crucified (Scorp. c.

---

scriptores quidquam indicare potuerint, ex quo veritatis umbra saltem aliqua appareat. Nec certi quidquam statui posse arbitror de illorum ordine et successione."—COSSART, i. 6.

These quotations are from the writings of two celebrated Jesuits.

ult.), we must not lose sight of the writings, published under the names of Linus, Marcellus, and Denis the Areopagite, which were at that time circulated so numerously, and which seduced even the good faith of the venerable fathers of the Church. We have just seen, as regards the ordination of Clement, the contradictory opinion of Tertullian as to his being the *first* Bishop of Rome. But this is by no means the only instance in which he states facts entirely unknown to his predecessors. According to him, not only was St. Peter at Rome, but St. John also laboured there, and was there condemned to death; but, though thrown into a barrel of boiling water, escaped death, and was afterwards banished. St. Jerome repeats this history, but takes good care to decline the responsibility of it, and refers it simply to the authority of Tertullian. It is, moreover, clear, that the Church of Rome has not dared at any time to certify this narrative of Tertullian, and, in refusing to do so, has given a striking proof of the little confidence due to this Father in matters connected with history. Now, the martyrdom of Peter and that of John are related simultaneously; historical criticism has, therefore, a just right to reject both facts, since the falsity of one is clearly evident, and the reality of the other rests on a like foundation in authority.

Eusebius, in order to maintain the fact of the martyrdom of St. Peter and St. Paul, cites (ii. 24) the testimony of Gaius, who was a priest of Rome towards the year 200, under the Pope Zephyrine. The writing of this priest, " Adversum Proculum, Patronum Cataphrygarum," contains the following passage: " Ego vero Apostolorum tropæa ostendere possum. Nam sive in Vaticanum, sive ad Ostiensem viam pergere licet, occurrunt tibi tropæa eorum, qui ecclesiam illam fundaverunt."

Even supposing these words to be authentic, there are two observations which we have to make concerning them, which greatly compromise the importance and credibility of the declaration of Gaius.

1st. There is only a vague mention of *Apostles*. Under this title, not only Apostles properly so called, but also their disciples and fellow-labourers were often comprised. We see in the New Testament this title given to Titus, Timothy, Silas, Barnabas, &c.; and in Clement of Alexandria (Stromata, iv. 17), Clement of Rome is honoured with the same distinction. The words of Gaius, therefore, prove nothing in favour of the tradition concerning St. Peter. On the contrary, they make against it. "EORUM *qui ecclesiam illam fundaverunt*" reminds us rather of St. Paul and his fellow-labourers, whom he so often mentions, and to whom one is more naturally led to attribute the establishment and oversight of the first Roman church.

2d. Whatever may be the true sense of the word *tropæa*, as M. Ellendorf remarks, it is more than probable, that in these times of persecution against every thing that savoured of Christianity, —at this period of extreme hatred to the progress of evangelical doctrine, there could not have been, close to the Vatican, close to the tombs of the Scipios, and on the road of Ostia, exposed to the public gaze, monuments and inscriptions in honour and commemoration of the Apostles.

Origen, the last of the Fathers of the Church whom we shall quote on this part of our subject, goes much farther in his account of the life of St. Peter. He relates, in a quotation by Eusebius, iii. 1, that St. Peter arrived at Rome towards the end of his life (επι τελει), and was there crucified with his head downwards. The influence of the "Passio Petri" of the Pseudo-Linus* is here recognised, as M. Ellendorf remarks.

But how shall we make this passage of Origen, quoted by Eusebius, harmonise with other accounts given by the same historian, who elsewhere declares, that St. Peter came to Rome in the second year of the reign of Claudius, and with the relation of Lactantius, who places this event a little while after the advent of Nero to the throne?

In short, the more the times advance, the more these legends enlarge: fictions become exaggerated, errors multiply, chaos augments, and criticism is embarrassed.

We have now arrived, in this historical investigation, midway in the third century, and we will there stop. It were perfectly useless to add name to name of those who, since this period, have given testimony of their faith in the fact which we call in question.

---

* Ruffin, in his translation of the " Ecclesiastical History of the Bishop of Cesarea," adds, upon his *own authority*, as must be conjectured, another circumstance, viz. that St. Peter had himself *demanded* this kind of punishment, as counting himself unworthy to suffer the same death as the Lord.

The result of our researches on the tradition of the first ages amounts, then, to this:—

Nothing that we can find has clearly proved, so as entirely to place it beyond the reach of suspicion, any prolonged residence of St. Peter at Rome. None of the testimonies generally quoted by the defenders of the Romish Church is exempt, as we think we have shewn, from corruption. They all give place to doubt and dispute as to the sense imposed upon them by that Church.

The ecclesiastical authors of the first, of the second, and of the first half of the third century do not firmly sustain the Romish opinion; for some, as, for instance, Clement of Rome, Ignatius, Polycarp, Justin, Hermas, Hegesippus, are entirely silent as to the asserted residence of St. Peter at Rome; and others, such as Clement of Alexandria, Papias, Tertullian, and Origen, have either suffered themselves to be led into error, or are not generally worthy of any historical faith.

The only fact which we can admit as *possible*, because negative proofs against it fail, is the arrival of the Apostle Peter at Rome towards the

end of his life, and his martyrdom under Nero.*
But, at the same time, it must be clearly understood, that the proofs which have been extracted as *positive*, from the testimony of ecclesiastical writers, by no means affirm it.

Guided by the indications or the silence of the Bible, considering the twilight in which human passions and infirmities have obscured the Apostolic times, appreciating at their just value the causes which have availed to lead all Christendom into such a faith, the historian as well as the Christian, faithful to the instructions of the Gospel and even of tradition itself, ought to repulse, without hesitation, the opinion that makes St. Peter reside, for a space of twenty-five years, in the

---

* Several moderate Romanists go no farther than Origen in their suppositions relative to the journey of St. Peter to Rome. We would cite, amongst these, an article inserted in a German Roman Catholic review, entitled, "Tübinger Katholische Quartalschrift, 1830," fourth number, p. 612. Theod. Beza thus expresses himself, relative to the common tradition on St. Peter: "Quod traditum est de viginti quinque illis annis, quibus Petrus Romæ sederit, partim ex Pauli epistolis Roma scriptis probabiliter refellitur, partim etiam necessariis argumentis demonstratur ex temporum supputatione; etiamsi Romam illum venisse ibique pro Christi nomine trucidatum fuisse, non invitus concedam."

present capital of the Roman Catholic world, as Bishop of Rome and chief of the Church universal. "Is it to be credited," says Dr. Malan of Geneva, "that one hundred and fifty years should elapse from the death of St. Peter, and yet all history, during that period, be silent, either as to his visit to Rome or his bishopric? It is Papias, that mind fruitful in visionary doctrine, who, towards the end of the second century, conceives the recital of it, and because that Irenæus repeats it, without any other authority, it is received and worshipped."

Let those, then, who have followed our reasonings attentively and honestly judge the following passage of Valesius (*ad Euseb.* ii. 15) : "Atque nihil in tota historia ecclesiastica illustrius, nihil *certius* atque *testatius* quam adventus Petri Apostoli in urbem Romanam." Let them also decide concerning the validity of Scaliger's assertion, "Can any one who has the least acquaintance with literature admit what is said concerning the journey of St. Peter to Rome, or his residence of twenty-five years in that city, or the martyrdom that he there suffered?" (in Johan. xviii. 31.)

Apart from the Bible and from tradition, many arguments not less available might be found in an elaborate, scrupulous, and correct study of the exterior history of the Primitive Church; but this, for the present, we abandon to others better qualified for the task, and conclude with the following reflection:

What ought we to think of this multiformity of legend concerning St. Peter, and of the numerous discrepancies of ancient authors, both as to the epoch of his arrival at Rome and the year of his death? The same writer, Eusebius, makes him come to Rome, first in the second year of the reign of Claudius, and secondly, on the testimony of Origen, towards the end of his life. Lactantius asserts that it was under Nero; the "Liber Pontificalis," falsely attributed to Pope Damasus, the first year of the reign of this emperor; Onuphrius, in 69; the "Pseudo-Dexter," in 66.

The death of the Apostle has been, as we have also seen, the subject of many varying accounts.*

---

* *The most ancient catalogue of the Popes*, inserted in the "Fastes" of Cuspinian, and in the "Commentary on the Paschal Canon of Gilles Bucher," *fixes the* DEATH *of the Apostle St. Peter to the first year of the reign of Nero, which was the fifty-fourth of our Lord.* This is the remark which Spanheim makes in his treatise entitled "De ficta

Even the simultaneousness of his martyrdom with that of St. Paul has been questioned both by Prudens and Augustine; and in order to put an end to this burdensome controversy, a categorical declaration of the Roman synod assembled under Pope Gelasius became necessary, wherein it was enounced, "Uno tempore uno eodemque die gloriosa morte cum Petro in urbe Roma sub Nerone agonizans coronatus est."

These contradictions, which might be made

Profectione Petri Apostoli in urbem Romam deque non una traditionis origine," 1679.—*Opp.* tom i. Lugd. Batav. 1703, p. 331.

"Concerning the time of St. Peter's coming to Rome," says Fulke, "the ancient writers do not agree. Eusebius saith it was in the time of Claudius; but Hierom saith he sat there twenty-five years, until the last year of Nero: it must follow that he came thither the second or third of Claudius. Yet Damasus saith he came to Rome in the beginning of Nero's empire, and sat there twenty-five years; whereas, Nero reigned but fourteen years. He saith, also, that his disputation with Simon Magus was in the presence of Nero the Emperor. Eusebius reporteth it under Claudius. Anterius, bishop of Rome, as Nicephorus testifieth, did write that Peter was translated from Antioch to Rome, and from thence he passed to Alexandria, because he might more profit the Church there."— FULKE's *Confutation of the Rhenish Annotators*, quoted in Elliott's "Delineation of Romanism."—TRANSLATOR.

more evident were other details entered into, confirm the maxim "that fables always destroy each other."

2. In a discussion which arose in the second century on a question of ceremonies, and during the conference of St. Polycarp, bishop of Smyrna, with Anicetus, bishop of Rome,* Polycarp availed himself of the authority of the Apostle John, and of the other Apostles with whom he had conversed. Far from opposing to him the authority of the Prince of the Apostles, the Chief of the Church, which would have been, could he have adduced it, unanswerable, Anicetus simply appealed to the custom of the *elders who had preceded him* (τὴν συνήθειαν τῶν πρὸ αὐτοῦ πρεσβυτέρων).† Was the twelfth ‡ Bishop of Rome, then, ignorant of the eminent advantages of his position ? Was he ignorant of the fact that he was the successor of St. Peter ? Did he not know that Polycarp was greatly his inferior, as being no more than the

---

* This conference took place, according to some, in the year 152; according to others, as, for instance, Pagi, in 158.

† Irenæus, cited by Eusebius, v. 24.

‡ According to Malebranche and others, Anicetus was the eleventh Bishop of Rome, including St. Peter.

disciple and successor of St. John? Must we conclude from this that the legend we have discussed was not yet invented, or, at least accredited, in the time of Anicetus?

3. The tombs of St. Peter and St. Paul at Rome, upon which basilicas and churches more magnificent than the palaces of emperors have been erected, and whither the people crowded with zeal and reverence in the times of Augustine, Jerome, and Chrysostom, are for many Romanists a positive proof of the residence of these Apostles in the city of Rome. This proof is forcibly repudiated by a French author, whose words we here quote.*

"At this monumental testimony I could not refrain from smiling; for if we are to believe that saints have died in all the places where their tombs are preserved, we shall have to believe that they have died several times over, since the tombs of the same saint are shewn in many places. The body of St. Andrew is worshipped at Constantinople, at Amalfi, at Toulouse, in Russia, at the convent of the Apostles in Armenia, without reck-

* ANDRÉ BLANC, "De la Pretendue Primauté du Pape et du Séjour de St. Pierre à Rome, en réponse à M. l'Abbé Tabardel." Paris, 1838, p. 40.

EXAMINATION OF THE TRADITION. 115

oning a sixth head of the Apostle, which may be devoutly kissed at Rome. The body of St. James is venerated at Compostella, at Verona, at Toulouse, at Pistoie, at Rome, without mentioning a sixth head of the saint which is carried in procession at Venice, and a seventh, which is preserved in the abbey of St. Wasth at Arras. There are eight bodies of St. Luke the Evangelist, eighteen bodies of St. Paul, thirty bodies of St. Pancratius in as many different cities, whilst I should need time and space to reckon up all the relics of St. Peter. Formerly Constantinople claimed to have possession of his body, except the head, which was left at Rome. Very considerable relics of this saint are venerated in the abbey of Claude, in Franche-Comté, in the convent of Cluny, and at Arles. There is a finger at the monastery of the *three churches* in Armenia, a thumb at Toulon, three teeth at Marseilles, an entire jaw, with the beard, at Poitiers.

"It is not only for the establishment of the primacy of St. Peter that his tomb is preserved at Rome; it is also to put the credulity of the simple to profit, and prey upon the purses of the poor pilgrims. First of all, those who descend into the holy cell which contains the precious relic, gain seven years' indulgence for every step,* and it is well known that these indulgences must be paid for in ready money. The oil of a hundred silver lamps, which burn without ceasing around the tomb, gives sight to the blind; and this is paid for, doubtless, with a good round sum. The holy father is careful to place on the sacred tomb the *pallium*, or archiepiscopal mantle, destined for newly ordained archbishops, who are required to cause this precious ornament to be demanded by procuration and kneeling, *instanter, instantius, instantissime* — that is to say, earnestly, more earnestly, most earnestly — in the three months of their nomination, under pain of being deprived of their dignity.† This pious traffic brings every year a revenue of about a hundred thousand ducats into the coffers of the ' poor *servant of the servants of Jesus Christ.*' "

In keeping with this passage, what Lady Morgan has recounted on the subject of the *Festa di Cattedra* at Rome, or the commemoration of the installation of the see of St. Peter, celebrated every 18th January, will be read with interest.

* " Misson," tom. ii. p. 129.

† Durand de Maillaine, " Dictionn. de Droit Canon," under the word *Pallium*.

"At the extremity of the great nave behind the altar, and mounted on a tribune designed or ornamented by Michael Angelo, stands a sort of throne, composed of precious materials, and supported by four gigantic figures. A glory of seraphim, with groups of angels, sheds a brilliant light upon its splendours. This throne enshrines the real, plain, worm-eaten, wooden chair on which St. Peter, the prince of the Apostles, is said to have pontificated: more precious than all the bronze, gold, and gems with which it is hidden, not only from impious but from holy eyes, and which once only in the flight of ages was profaned by mortal inspection.

"The sacrilegious curiosity of the French broke through all obstacles to their seeing the chair of St. Peter. They actually removed its superb casket, and discovered the relic. Upon its mouldering and dusty surface were traced carvings which bore the appearance of letters. The chair was quickly brought into a better light, the dust and cobwebs removed, and the inscription (for an inscription it was) faithfully copied. The writing is in Arabic characters, and is the well-known confession of Mahometan faith, *There is but one God, and Mahomet is his prophet!*' It is sup-

118   EXAMINATION OF THE TRADITION.

posed that this chair had been among the spoils of the Crusaders, offered to the Church at a time when a taste for antiquarian lore and the deciphering of inscriptions were not yet in fashion. This story has since been hushed up, the chair replaced, and none but the unhallowed remember the fact, and none but the audacious repeat it. Yet such there are, even at Rome!"*

---

* "Italy," by Lady Morgan.

There is another account, sufficiently curious, of this chair given in Elliott's "Delineation of Romanism," edited by the Rev. J. Stamp, p. 636. It is there said, that "the prelates of Rome had, as they thought, till the year 1662, sufficient proof that the chair was erected by Peter, and that he sat thereon. Till that period the chair was exposed annually on the 18th January, the festival of the said chair, for public adoration. While it was cleaning, in order to be set up in some conspicuous place in the Vatican, the twelve labours of Hercules unluckily appeared carved upon it. Giacomo Bartolini, who was present at the discovery, affirms that their worship was not misplaced, since it was paid not to the wood but to the Prince of the Apostles. Another distinguished author, unwilling to surrender the worship of the chair, attempted to explain the labours of Hercules in a mystical sense — namely, as emblematical of the future exploits of the popes!" If both these accounts are true, it is evident that there have been at least two chairs exhibited, each as identically the chair which St. Peter used.—TRANSLATOR.

CHAPTER IV.

ORIGIN OF THE ROMISH TRADITION CONCERNING ST. PETER.

NOTWITHSTANDING the probability of all the arguments which have just been adduced against the asserted abode of St. Peter at Rome, it seems clear, however, that there must have been some positive and indisputable fact for the foundation of a legend so generally credited and received during so many centuries throughout Christendom.

This is an objection which will naturally suggest itself to the minds of those who are not familiar with the records of ecclesiastical antiquity. It is one which we ought to expect, and our answer to it is this: —

The conclusion that is drawn from this universal faith in testimony to the tradition in question is, though of apparent weight, really valueless. Its nullity has been recognised in very many circumstances where historical truth has been found in manifest opposition to common belief. In proof of this we will cite some instances of discordance between faith and fact.

In our own day an image of the Virgin Mary is worshipped at Madrid under the name of the Holy Virgin of Atocha. This image, according to the account given by Metaphrastes, was brought by St. Peter himself from the city of Antioch, asserted to be the seat of his first bishopric. St. Peter, however, was never Bishop of Antioch, and what is still more evident, nothing can be found in his writings to countenance the worship of Mary.

St. John was never at Rome, notwithstanding that Tertullian and a crowd of others, as well as the compilers of the Breviary, have asserted it. They were all the dupes of the imagination of a Pseudo-Prochorus.

How many millions have made the pilgrimage to the tomb of St. James of Compostella? St. James was beheaded in the year 45 by the orders of Herod, without ever having set foot in Spain.

The Romish Church has set apart special days

for celebrating the fêtes of the immaculate Conception and the Assumption of the Blessed Virgin. Now it must be manifest to any one who has the least knowledge of things divine, that these two facts are not only unknown to the sacred writers of the Scriptures, but diametrically opposed to the spirit of all which they wrote. The doctrine of the *maculate conception* was preached by the most renowned doctors of the middle ages, as, for instance, by St. Bernard, in whose time the contrary doctrine was proclaimed, to the great indignation of the Abbot of Clairvaux. In 1507 four Dominicans, who defended the same proposition, though in an unworthy and disreputable manner, against the Order of the Franciscans, suffered death at the stake. Pope Sixtus IV., who felt himself unable to repress the attacks which were directed against the dogma sanctioned by the Council of Bâle, formally authorised in 1476 the free discussion of this subject of controversy. Notwithstanding all this, the idolatrous worship of the immaculate Virgin still obtained and prospered, although she was, according to the confession of St. Augustine, born in sin, *ex concupiscentia nata ;* and men do not hesitate now to declare in the pulpit that the worship of Mary is that which must revivify religious sentiment in philosophic France. The Abbé P. C. D——, Professor of Theology at the College Stanislas, says, "My conviction is that the worship of Mary will save the present generation, as it has formerly saved our fathers." —*La Chaire Catholique.* Paris, 1845. Livraison d'Avril.

Lastly (and this directly bears upon the subject), the Romish church lies prostrate at the foot of a statue of St. Peter at Rome. "Now, unfortunately, this statue of St. Peter is neither more nor less, according to the acknowledgment of the learned, and even of the cardinals, than a statue of Jupiter. So that mischance multiplies in the whole affair, and the very fact becomes a true type of the tradition concerning St. Peter. He was Bishop of Rome as surely as that this statue is his." *

As to the immense influence which this belief in St. Peter's residence at Rome has acquired in the Roman Catholic world, as to the tone of conviction with which it is sustained by the ultra-Montanists, there can be no mistake, and there should be no misgiving. Every one who is blindly devoted to a system of priestly tyranny, all the

* A. Bost, p. 108.

mercenaries and false disciples of pontifical power, will take good heed how they shake a faith on which the colossus that they worship is seated. In order to maintain it they will torture texts till they become favourable, invent and embellish legends, falsify the documents that are opposed, and leave no means untried by which they may fascinate the ignorant devotee.

It must not be thought that enlightened and sincere Romanists have never, in the depths of their own conscience and the confidence of their familiar intercourse with each other, called in question the Roman episcopate of St. Peter. There are not many of them, it is true, who have had the courage to approach this difficult subject with the freedom that distinguished the learned M. Ellendorf, who, nevertheless, was Roman Catholic in heart and in faith. The necessary erudition for quoting other authors of the same profession, who have declared or implied the same opinion as that which we have enounced, fails us; but some there are, although their number is doubtless small. The members of the Romish clergy, desirous of maintaining peace with the court of Rome, must find it in every way preferable to follow the pacific precept which M. de

Maistre has given them, when treating of the attacks directed by Protestants or Gallicans against the infallibility of the Pope. "To write against this magnificent and divine privilege of the chair of St. Peter is a position most unworthy of a Catholic, and even of a man of the world. As to the priest who allows himself in such an abuse of his intellect and learning, he is blind, and even, if I do not infinitely mistake, derogates from his character. Even he, be his profession what it may, who hesitates concerning the theory, ought always to recognise the fact, and confess that the sovereign pontiff can never err. He ought at least to yield his heart to this faith, if he cannot logically assent to it as a proposition, instead of degrading himself to a schoolman's cavil in order to shake it."*

---

* *Du Pape*. M. de Tillemont is yet more *naïf* when speaking concerning the fables which have been uttered of Simon the Sorcerer. He says, "Supposing it to be true that this history is a fiction, we prefer, so long as its falsehood is not clearly demonstrated, to err with Arnobius, St. Cyril of Jerusalem, the legates of Pope Liberius, St. Ambrose, St. Augustine, St. Isidore of Pelusia, Theodoret, and several others, than to be compelled to yield to the idea that a great number of the most illustrious and gravest masters of the Church, both Greek and Latin, had been guilty of an indiscreet credulity."

In the earliest ages of Christianity we meet with many Fathers of the Church who are as much opposed to ambitious pretensions as to subversive heresies : we see several of them contending against the idea of any superiority, whether of Peter over his colleagues, or of Rome over other Apostolic sees. Gregory the Great himself, at the end of the sixth century, is yet sufficiently honest to qualify as *diabolical* and *anti-Christian* the title of universal bishop assumed by the Patriarchs of Constantinople.* In the times in which we live, ultra-Montanist writers dare no longer acknowledge the absence of historical and positive proof concerning the episcopal functions of St. Peter in the present residence of the Holy Fathers. The divisions brought in by the great events of the sixteenth century, and the schismatic movements of the last year, render this acknowledgment too dangerous. Notwithstanding that the reality of the office and functions attributed to St. Peter has been contested for the last three centuries by Protestants of all kinds, by Jansenists and far-famed philologists, yet, in despite of reiterated attacks, the valiant champions of the

---

* Epist. i. 7, 27, ad Athana. ; v. 19, ad Sabiniam.

Papacy, such as De Maistre, Zeloni, and the Bishop of Liege, who have all treated controversially the subject of the Romish primacy, have rapidly passed over the historical fact of St. Peter's abode at Rome as ground too dangerous to rest upon. They have confined themselves to a direct and sequential refutation of the objections raised against the pretensions of Rome, limiting themselves to reasonings purely theological, and avoiding as far as possible any examination of the historical evidence of the fact upon which those pretensions are based. Over this unlucky subject the historians of the Romish church glide with equal facility: even the prolixity of Tillemont is at fault, whilst Fleury innocently repeats " the opinions of his Fathers." The antiquity of the belief, and the tranquillity which the adherents of the Papacy manifest under attack, are not in themselves any guarantee of the solidity of the Romish claim to the primacy.

What, then, is the true source, the ultimate and real ground of this fiction? What are the circumstances which have given birth, which have nourished it, which even in our own times nourish it still? We will attempt to answer this question.

It must not be forgotten, however, that in so

doing we approach a subject surrounded with difficulties, which increase exactly in proportion as the spirit of truth, animating the immediate disciples our Lord, becomes weakened and defiled. The earlier ages of Christianity gave birth to the fictions of visionary imaginations, to the illusions of an unintelligent piety, and to the results of artificial and fleshly combinations. The moment Christian men elevated these to the rank of absolute verities, which it was both useful and necessary for the interests of Christianity to esteem and maintain, historic truth became involved in a labyrinth of human inventions, more or less fraudulent, so as scarcely to be perceived in the obscurity that surrounded it.

Christian antiquity has its *mythes* as well as that of Greece and Rome, and its traditions, at once instructive and fascinating. The spirit of man, limited as it is, has always been disposed to lend material forms to ideas of the infinite — to humanise things divine, and to individualise general facts.

Abstract truth can only be impressed on ordinary minds through the medium of the feelings, and these need for their nourishment the constant occurrence of sensible and palpable facts. The introduction of Christianity, in developing an entirely new sphere of ideas, opposed in every way to those which gave life to the fallen civilisation, must have created much enthusiasm; even the joy naturally consequent upon the reception of its truths became, in some instances, excitement. These very early led Christians to receive as true, without a scrupulous examination, whatever was calculated to increase the splendour, to manifest the mystic virtues, and to assure the success of the doctrines of the Gospel. Moreover, the recollections and ceremonies of Paganism were not extinct; and as the pure simplicity of evangelical truth yielded before the corruption that supervened, amalgamation with the errors of heathenism, or imitation of its fabulous and mystic rites, was the consequence. Jupiter, the personification of supreme power, had been seen surrounded by the numerous and brilliant court of Olympus; it was hardly to be wondered at that the Christian world, yielding to the mournful and deceitful influence of royal protection, and dazzled by the pomp of Rome and of the East, which had been introduced into the Church, should have merged the humility of Christianity in the pageantry of power, and attached to the lowly presence of the gentle Jesus a *cortège* of saints and virgins, of bishops and popes, priests and acolytes, in all the pride of hierarchical dignity, until, at length, Christianity as well as heathenism numbered its demigods, and the weak and rude intelligence of these ages yielded to the fascination of a mythical system, the mysterious offspring of truth and error, piety and human infirmity.

Amongst the Christian doctors of this epoch there were some who recognised and acknowledged that which was fabulous, but tolerated it as an excellent means for bringing the souls of men under the power of the Gospel. Others, instead of suppressing it, exaggerated and accredited it, guided in that which they did by an ardour that was sometimes pious, but more often culpable. Others, again, indeed opposed the error, but felt it difficult to overthrow it by an enlightened exposition of the Holy Scriptures — a difficulty which has ever proved an inherent vice in religious fanaticism, because of the limited and partial system of interpretation which such fanaticism engenders. On the other hand, the struggles of sectarianism found in the fabulous and in the false powerful instruments for the maintenance of their several claims. The generation that had possessed the privilege of hearing the voice of Apostles, passed away. Hegesippus, the first historian of the Church, began to write; and the insidious and impious conspiracy of error was constituted, finding its elements in the perfidy of those who substituted the declaration of truth by their own perverse doctrines.* Supposing the influence of this religious *mythe* to have been salutary upon the Christian feeling—supposing even these associations, so skilfully combined, to have been eminently successful in subjugating the civilised world by their fascinating power,—still the reasoning mind of the reflecting man, the feeling of the rational and evangelically religious, the assured and well-tried experience of modern generations, can never recognise these fictions, and the mournful consequences which they produced, as legitimate and sanctioned. They must always regard them as a culpable amalgamation of error with truth. The illusion of the mysterious yields before the progress of enlightenment; and, as a natural result, what was a *mythe* takes its true form, and becomes a *fable*. Now the very Apostle upon whom the Romish

---

* Heges. ap. Euseb. "Hist. Eccles." iii.

Church claims to be built condemns *fables*, and desires to banish them from the midst of those to whom he wrote (2 Peter, i. 16).

These general remarks have seemed to us necessary for the solution of the question that now specially occupies us.

The true psychological origin of the erroneous traditions which exist concerning St. Peter must be looked for in the manifest disposition of the earlier ages to surround the heroes of the Christian faith with a halo conformable to their greatness, and to glorify, in passing the limits of truth, the theatres of their Apostolic labours. As to the legend of the Roman bishopric of St. Peter, it is neither more nor less than the natural result of a tendency and desire for an external unity of all the faithful, and for the centralisation of the government of the Church in the metropolis of the empire—a tendency grounded upon a truth, which the Romish Church has perverted and falsified, which, emanating from a sincere piety, she has utilised for the purposes of her own ambition,* and which, consequently, has only

---

* "Before that the devil had introduced ambition into the Church, every thing in it was conducted by the college of

been fruitful in pernicious consequences, increasing in evil generation after generation.

It is not, however, an easy thing, as it has been already remarked, to treat the tradition concerning St. Peter in all its historic and literary bearing, to trace it to its source, analyse the causes of its birth and developement in the primitive times of Christianity. This would require minute attention to all the manifestations of religious influence, not only in its operation on the minds of individual men, but on the temporal and external condition of the Church at large. It would necessitate an elaborate study of, and deep investigation into, the nature of the struggle between Christianity and Heathenism, the strife of sect against sect within the pale of the Church, and the various dissensions which have separated heretical innovators from her orthodox communion.

Such a task as this hardly falls within our purpose; for the scrupulous examination of all that

elders."—AMBROS. in 1 *Tim.* i. 5; also HIERON. *Epist. I. ad Tur.* Dr. Bauer, in the collection entitled, "Tübinger Zeitschrift für Theologie" (1831, 4th number, p. 163), allows *dogmatic* reasons as having given birth to the supposition of the Roman Episcopate of St. Peter.

has been written on the subject which is proper to it would require more space and attention than the limits and design of this work would permit. After all, the authors whose writings we should have to examine are unworthy of confidence, the crowd of writings which would have to be considered for the most part apocryphal and forged, and it is but lost labour to reiterate criticism on documents whose falsity has been recognised and whose errors have been proved. Minds of greater capacity than ours, and every way better qualified for the task, have already undertaken it; and those who desire to see the question which we have here considered treated in the full extent of its literary and historic bearing, will do well to consult their works. After having demonstrated, in the first place, the silence of the Bible on the residence of St. Peter at Rome, and, in the second, the nullity of the evidence extracted from the Fathers of the Church, and generally alleged in favour of Romish opinion, the question, Who, then, has established this fact? may serve even as a valuable accessory in its refutation.

Where History is silent, Fable speaks; she seizes the ground which History has left uncultivated, and the epochs untrodden by the investigations of criticism. The very barrenness which exists in the absence of historic evidence is favourable to her growth and developement. In regions where calm reason has not trod, discussed, and judged — where, above all, Divine revelation (in whatever sense men understand it) has not spoken, man delights to create after his own image, and to invent at the pleasure of his imagination or his passions. But the creations of man are as perishable as himself, when they are not quickened by the breath of Him who is the source and preserver of life.

Hence the fervid imagination of Christians very early filled up the gaps which the authors of the Holy Scriptures had left in their historic record, gave consistency and arrangement to its own productions, joined them to the writings of the Apostles, surrounded the facts connected with the life and suffering of our blessed Lord (in themselves so simple and grand) with an immense labyrinth of useless details, and finished by stifling the spiritual germ of evangelical truth under sensual elements—by obscuring its quickening spirit under forms which, however fair to outward seeming, were repressive of life.

The Apostle Peter, once eclipsed by the great

Missionary of the Gentiles, disappeared, as we have seen, from the record of Scripture. Immediately all that concerned him became the subject of fabulous invention, taking in its birth the impress of the intention, pure or culpable, which originated it. It cannot be doubted that there was plenty of room for the exaggerations of a fervent piety, even for the suggestions of flattery and ambition. The Apocryphal writers, who were the principal inventors or propagators of the fabulous legends of Christianity, had, from the council of Jerusalem to the death of Peter under Nero, towards 67, sufficient space and opportunity for giving full scope to their pious imaginings.

Time would fail us to cite the numerous authors who, in the consciousness of their own weakness, borrowed the honourable names of Linus, of Clement, of Prochorus, and even of the Apostles themselves; time would fail us to enumerate the multitude of *Epistles*, of *Passions*, of *Gospels*, of *Recognitions*, of *Constitutions*, and of *Canons*, which inundated the second century, and constituted the Christian literature of that period. Those who are curious in this matter we would refer to a work recently published, entitled, " Roman Forgeries and Falsifications; or, An Examination of

Counterfeit and Corrupted Records, with especial reference to Popery," by the Rev. Richard Gibbings, M.A.

The fabulous history concerning St. Peter once established and propagated,* the Romish Church immediately availed herself of it for the maintenance of her own ambitious projects, for the support of her power, and for the advancement of her progress in the false direction which she had taken. From this period the question concerning St. Peter has ever been closely connected with the establishment of the Romish hierarchy and the doctrine of Romish supremacy. In the course of the third century the bishop of Rome, sustained by a considerable party of ecclesiastical chiefs, aspired to the primacy. It became absolutely necessary, for the establishment and consolidation of the external unity which was contemplated,

* The works published under the names of Linus and Denis the Areopagite are principally those which contain the *mythe* on St. Peter. Their narratives were collected together, reformed, and enlarged in the tenth century by Simon Metaphrastes, the famous Martyrologist of Byzantium. Lactantius, lib. iv. c. 21, would lead us to suppose that the book of the *preaching* of St. Peter, often cited by Clement of Alexandria, and composed in the time of Paphias, has had no small share in originating the legend of which we treat.

that two facts should be verified: these facts were the supremacy of Simon Peter over the other Apostles, and the presence of this Apostle in the capital of the world as bishop and founder of the Christian Church in that city; and it was not difficult, by a forced interpretation of some isolated passages in the Scripture, to give them the appearance of truth. It was at this time that the fable lost its character of poetic reverie, acquired consistency, was elevated into a reality—the base of a monstrous power, and became the mighty instrument of a formidable hierarchy.*

In point of fact, the whole Roman theocracy, in all its extent and bearing, rests simply and entirely on the asserted primacy of St. Peter and on his Roman Bishopric. The *first* is not only

---

* The Pseudo-Denis, in one of his writings which the Romish Church esteems, *instructs* us very clearly as to the use that was made of popular belief. "Those," he says, "to whom Jesus Christ confided the care of establishing and ruling the hierarchy of the Church have rightly chosen sensible things in order to express and figure the things which are above the senses. They knew that our nature, so dependent in every way upon the senses, needed to be struck and held through the medium of these very senses, in order to be raised to the height of things purely intellectual."—Vide GUILLON, *Bibliothèque des Pères de l'Eglise*, tom. xx. p. 480 (edition of Louvain).

contested by the testimony of Scripture, but is totally unknown to the earlier Fathers of the Church :* whilst the *second* is only supported by the evidence of some apocryphal or credulous writers. Passing altogether by the spirit of the Gospel, and consulting only temporal, or at least temporary interests, the following proposition is asserted, without satisfactory evidence of any kind, as an indisputable fact, "Peter is the only foundation-stone of the Church, his Roman see is the centre of life and activity to all the members of this body, one and indivisible, his successors are the sole depositories and dispensers of the graces and gifts of the Christian faith." Hence it has now become an indisputable dogma. "*Primatus Petro datur, ut una Christi ecclesia et cathedra una monstretur.*" (Cyprian.)

It is useless to bring to light the motives, manifest or secret, which urge the spiritual conductors of the Roman Catholic world to sustain so vigorously the vulgar tradition concerning

---

* Vide Cyprian, who is not always very consistent; he says, "All the Apostles were like St. Peter clothed with the same honour and with the same authority :" "*Hoc erant utique et ceteri Apostoli quod fuit Petrus pari, consortio præditi et honoris et potestatis.*"—*De Unitat. Ecclesiæ.*

St. Peter. Without doubt they will always proclaim, *"for the salvation of souls,"* the impregnable credibility of the false assertions of Eusebius. As we, however, desire to search only into the simple truth, and believe it perfectly possible to follow the Lord Jesus Christ without following the Pope, we do not hesitate to declare, with the record of history in hand, that the prolonged residence of St. Peter at Rome, and his labours in that city in quality of bishop universal, is a pure invention of theological mythology, of which the Papal policy has skilfully availed itself, in order to arrive at that supremacy, towards which, if we do not greatly mistake, the irresistible course of human events necessarily urged it in certain times and under certain circumstances.

Whatever has been the duration of the error, it ought notwithstanding, being an error, to be rejected by him who, according to the divine precept, would worship God in *spirit and in truth*, and we cannot do better, in bringing these considerations to a close, than close them in the words of St. Augustine: *" Hic est mos diabolus, ut per antiquitatis traducem commendetur fallacia, possunt etiam latrones et adulteri pro se antiquitatem adferre."*

www.ingramcontent.com/pod-product-compliance
Lightning Source LLC
Chambersburg PA
CBHW050808160426
43192CB00010B/1682